Come Out of the Prison of Your Mind

MENTAL
KIDNAPPING II

GOD'S MENTAL THERAPY

Come Out of the Prison of Your Mind

MENTAL KIDNAPPING II

GOD'S MENTAL THERAPY

STEVEN TREADWELL

ARPress
ILLUMINATING IDEAS
EMPOWERING VOICES

ARPress
45 Dan Road Suite 36
Canton MA 02021

Hotline: 1(800) 220-7660
Fax: 1(855) 752-6001

Ordering Information:
Quantity Sales. Special discounts are available on quantity purchases by corporations, associations, and others. For details, contact the publisher at the address above.

Printed in the United States of America.

ISBN-13   Softcover   979-8-89330-885-3
             eBook   979-8-89330-886-0

Library of Congress Control Number: 2024902934

CONTENTS

PREFACE

When you read the title of my previous book, *Mental Kidnapping*, conversation had already started in your mind. *Mental Kidnapping II* will help you emancipate yourself from mental slavery, manipulation by mind therapy, and compartmentalizing.

I promise not to leave you alone until my book accomplishes what it set out to do—bring you back to your creator. I am seated with Christ in heavenly places dispatching my angels sending them to the north, south, east, and west to bring in the lost of this world to turn from Satan to Jehovah God. This is so they can have the peace of mind that Jesus Christ died and rose from the grave for.

Mental Kidnapping II: Mind Therapy is my trumpet to sound the alarm and fight the enemy to bring social wellness and awareness. It will help you remember your God as you stay fixed on his purpose for your life. I do this because it is never wrong to do the right thing.

"Rise up in me Lord God and scatter my enemies. Make those who hate you run from you" (Numbers 10:5). That's right. Every spirit contrary to my Jehovah God needs to get booking now in the mighty name of Jesus Christ. I call the angels of the Lord who are messengers swift as the wind, servants made of flaming fire, to surround you and the world. I decree and declare that you receive the Word coming forth so it and God will be alive and working in you.

Our young want to go back in time and be savage beasts, but we are all one blood. Whatever our races or sexes, we all still have the same blood. Jesus said, "How can you say that you love me whom you have not seen, and hate your brother that you see every day?" Satan twisted the thoughts of humankind in the beginning. Let's get back to

Eden, where man and woman began with God, and stop worshipping what God has created including Satan.

Adam and Eve were kicked out of the garden because they were hardheaded, rebellious, and disobedient. They did not submit to God totally. On God's solid rock I stand; all other grounds are sinking sands.

Wherever I land, it will be on God's Word or his will. There was a separation of blacks when some went the wrong way through the Strait of Gibraltar and ended up in the Caucasian Mountains in caves, but that is a whole different book on race. This is another book of how a black man turned white from the lack of melanin in his skin and became Caucasian. "The end is formed at the beginning." Genesis reveals that one man was formed from the dust of the ground and one woman from the rib of that man. God said in Acts 10:28, "But God hath shewed me that I should not call any man common or unclean." Our society is compartmentalizing itself by blocking out and putting the truth or a lie on the shelf just to be alone. We are all one blood. "And hath made of one blood all nations of men for to dwell on all the face of the earth, and hath determined the times before appointed, and the bounds of their habitation."

Manipulation in the form of voodoo, hoodoo, and witchcraft is running rampart in our daily lives. These people are trapped by their sins. Thank Jehovah for carrying and correcting us like children. Thank Jehovah's Holy Spirit who is in me, on me, around me, and for me. There is so much evil in the world, but God's people are standing tall through it all. God guided Israel to the Promised Land through all its enemies. It was black on black then in Egypt, and it is the same today in America. The spirit of witchcraft and sorcery is at its peak. I thank God that I am in the world but not of the world. I am taking up my cross, my sacrifice, and I hope the Lord God will find it acceptable in Jesus's name. His truth is marching on in me, amen.

"No one can say ; I am innocent; I have never done anything wrong" (Proverbs 20:9 Everyday Bible). God uses clean vessels. The Lord looks deep inside people and searches their thoughts. He is warning you that if you go back to your Egypt, from which he delivered you, you will die by war, hunger, or terrible disease. Pride means to show no respect toward God.

My child respects the Lord and the King, don't join those people who refuse to obey them, The Lord and King will quickly destroy such people. These two causes great disaster. (Proverbs 24:21–22 Everyday Bible)

When we spiritually consecrate ourselves to God, we dedicate our hearts to Him. We must reflect, repent, be baptized, separate ourselves from the world, and draw closer to God by staying committed to him. You can consecrate a person or a thing holy to the Lord; it is a personal act of dedication.

Consecrating ourselves is dedicating ourselves to a purpose or intention of the greatest importance. Right now, our nation is of the greatest importance. Let's get our leaders involved in prayer so we can pray together to our God. I see they are doing everything but praying, and prayer is what this world needs.

Prayer Covering

Heavenly Father, I pray this prayer by the power of the Holy Spirit and by the authority of the Word of God and the victory of Jesus Christ, the anointed one.

Lord Jesus, you died on the cross for my sins and rose from the dead. I am redeemed by your blood, and I belong to you. I confess all my sins known and unknown. I renounce these sins as well as those committed by my ancestors all the way back to the garden of Eden. I forgive them, myself, and everyone who has hurt me. Please forgive me and my ancestors. Cleanse me now from all curses and sin with your precious blood. As your servant, Lord Jesus, I put on the whole armor of God. I take the keys of the kingdom that have been given me as a believer, and I exercise the power that has been given to me to tread on serpents and scorpions and over all the power of the enemy.

I cover every area of my life with the blood of Jesus. I declare that nothing shall by any means hurt me. In the mighty name of Jesus Christ of Nazareth, I bind, rebuke, cast down, and bring to no effect all powers, principalities, evil forces, and spiritual wickedness in this world that is against me, my family, and those doing the work of God. I rebuke all evil and generational curses and disease, the powers of debt and lack, soul ties from sin, and all filthy communication and negative words coming out of people's mouths. I also break and render useless all prayers not inspired by the Holy Spirit that may have been placed against me in the mighty name of Jesus Christ.

Satan, you must flee from me now in terror. No weapon, no evil shall prosper against me. I am subject to God. I resist the devil so I can prosper my soul, body, spirit, and finances. Satan, get out of my life, mind, body, home, job, family, business dealings, finances, and all else that concerns me.

Father, I pray for your will to be done. I call forth my God-ordained destiny to materialize fully. I thank you, Father, that I stand firm in your spirit centering in on the gospel's work. I thank you, Father, that I have a godlyandlimitlessfaith.

I confess that I am called, anointed, and equipped to accomplish all God has called me to do. I overcome by the blood of the Lamb and the words of my testimony. I rebuke all rejection, bitterness, and rebellion. I put the blood of Jesus between me and these evil forces forever. I ask you, Lord, to dispatch mighty angels to protect and assist me.

I walk in forgiveness, Lord. I receive from you, Lord, my provider. I thank you, Lord, for divine appointment and open doors of opportunity. I call forth God-ordained increase and multiplication of souls. I declare it so in Jesus's mighty name. May the Lord perfect all that concerns me. Hallelujah!

(Ben and Malisa King, abbreviated version.)

CHAPTER 1

Manipulation

Is America Being Mentally Kidnapped?

We are so glad that we have found many cures for physical diseases. We can thank God for his Word for the healing and renewing of our minds. Our nation was built on the Word of God, but our salvation is built on the shed blood of Jesus Christ. We live only once, but if we do it right, once is enough.

I expect change because everything changes. Be big, better, and best. Be creative, and live out your imagination and creativity, not your history. Life is a stage, and you get only one performance, so make it a good one. There are no elevators to success. You must take the stairs one step at a time. Let the Word of God teach you how to open and get intimate with him. The greatest nation in the world is suffering from identity theft that began in the garden of Eden. Our country is running away from sound doctrine. The government wants to have full control of its citizens. Jehovah God wants you to have the mind of Christ and to hold the thoughts, feelings, and purposes of his heart. People are about to vote their way into slavery where they don't do what they want but only what the government wants. Government control will end only in sadness.

A house divided against itself cannot stand any more than a divided America can. The president says, "Either you are with me or against me. Either you are in or out." And most have been going out. "It's my way or the highway." And it seems the highway is jam-packed. Our country is getting gangrene from the inside, and God will have to cut the wickedness off. Our government wants to become a welfare state. It also has a taste of drug-induced amnesia caused by alcohol and pain medications and other illegal drugs that disturb mental functions.

Our society has a loss of memory regarding facts, information, and experiences. People can't seem to recall who they are. Loss of memory usually comes from aging or a concussion. Violent shaking in the relationships of our government in America has made families and leaders forget their roles. They are becoming unresponsive to their natural roles and are role-playing thanks to our government passing laws along with drugs, alcohol, and TV. Husbands and wives are divorcing and spending the rest of their lives trying to make each other miserable and destroy each other. Proverbs 23:7 says, "For as a man thinketh in his heart then so is he." You can't go any further than your thoughts take you. Others' thoughts seem to be on the curse and death, and the graveyard is not full.

Men and women are trying to win the best supporting actress award at the Oscars ceremony each year. Our government is supporting these actors as they help the LGBTQ+ agenda win Oscars as they play each other's roles. America's people are choosing roles as actors on a stage that has become Hollywood, which was around the corner from where I worked in California. I worked across from CBS on Beverly Boulevard, which was my first stop in the morning when I delivered flowers and baskets to the beauties of Hollywood. On my day off, I hung out at the basketball court at Roger Park right behind the DMV on Hyde Park Street in Inglewood, around the corner from where I lived. Hollywood is a place where anything that the mind can conceive can be done.

This state that we have come to that controls the public narrative is trying to strip away the norm that Jehovah set in place for man and woman. Satan is using the woman as a tool to divide and conquer. America is teaching second graders that drag queens are role models. Girls want to be boy scouts. Adults are raising their kids as nongender when God created onlymaleandfemale.

Certain women are openly rebelling against Jehovah by slapping him in the face with their choices. Everything God has, the devil has a counterfeit for. God told Israel to choose none of their ways. This does not reflect what the Bible teaches. When church denominations start supporting what is in the world, that becomes false Christianity. When you claim that the source of the world's agendas is Christ and the Bible, you are flogging. This is fake news.

This is real fake teaching that is brought to the children as adults place their imagination in children's minds. We must sound the trumpet. Jesus spoke about adultery and put a strict emphasis on looking and imagining. They mentally kidnap each other with tongues and tools they call toys to make believe they have the real *thang*.

God wanted to keep the Israelites away from the Sodomites and Amorites. He said to destroy that spirit completely because he did not want Israel or his children to be contaminated spiritually because that spirit was not of him. The Sodomites were professionals in sodomy. In "Lost" Angeles as I call it, sodomites have their own streets they hang out on. They wear jewels around their mouths, in their tongues, on their faces, and around their mouths advertising sodomy. They are the 2019 Sodomites. Call a spade a spade. If it walks like a duck and talks like a duck, it is a duck.

God wants us to be strong and very courageous. What are we going to say to that? We are put here to represent the Father and Jesus. We should tell the sodomites that they have the tools around their mouths that will send them straight to hell. They are not just minding their own business but interfering in mine by advertising their mouths painted and jeweled up ready for the act of sodomy. I can't tell a person what to wear because as soon as I come out my front door, I am public; I must deal with it. I am in the soul business.

God said in Ezekiel that we should set others' hearts on God. If I don't tell them, their blood will be on my head. If I tell them, their blood will be on their own heads. You are going to let me do my job, aren't you? I'm a watchman looking out for the souls of man and woman while I breathe God's fresh air.

People, listen. This is open rebellion against God. Show them in the Word of God—anywhere in the Old Testament—where God destroyed all the ones they are trying to betray. We must warn them that the road is out and they are about to go off the cliff. Don't be one of those people who won't tell even friends and family members that they have boogers in their noses. Now that's low down and dirty.

"You have heard that it was said to those of old, 'You shall not commit adultery' with her in his heart" (Matthew 27:28). The presence of drag queens is defiling and teaches others to rebel against Jehovah in their hearts. Some church leaders say the law is done away with, give deceptive interpretation of scriptures, and cause many to follow the lie. There are some things hard to understand.

> Who is it that does not understand? It is the untaught and unstable people who twist God's Word to their own destruction as they do also the rest of the Scriptures. Why are they confused? "You therefore beloved, since you know this beforehand, beware lest you also fall from your own steadfastness, being led away with the error of the wicked. (2 Peter 3:14–17)

Those who oppose God's laws will lead you away with fake Christianity. The inmates have taken over the asylum. Satan always wanted to be Jehovah. The enemy will have your child in school eight hours and bringing home polluted thoughts about their sexuality. Stay rooted in the Word to combat the fake news you will encounter. The apostle Paul warned the Ephesian elders,

> For I know this, that after my departure savage wolves will come in among you, not sparing the flock. Also, from among yourselves men will rise, speaking perverse things, to draw the disciples after themselves. (Acts 20:29–30)

The school system is being distorted with false accusations and fake news with the tools that were used against the followers of Christ then and now. Fake news, political correctness, and violence are not new. Jesus told us, "Blessed are you when they revile and persecute you and say all kinds of evil against you falsely for my sake" (Matthew 5:11). Jesus also warned us on the night he was betrayed that

> if the world hates you, you know that it hated Me before it hated you. If you were of the world, the world would love its own. Yet because you are not of the world, but I have chosen you out of the world, therefore the world hates you. (John 15:18–19)

This fake news started long ago, and it continues. This should not be a surprise to those who read the Bible.

There is a war against the Bible. We are choosing right now, and we need to find out right now who's on the Lord's side. There is secular pressure, pressure from media, and religious pressure, and we must choose this day whom we will serve. Paul warned those in Corinth about living licentious lives.

> Do you know that the unrighteous will not inherit the kingdom of God? Do not be deceived. Neither fornicators, nor idolaters, or adulterers, nor homosexuals, nor sodomites, will inherent the kingdom of God. (2 Corinthians 6:9–10)

This violent shaking in America has symptoms of amnesia, mild depression, stress, and persistent headaches causing a disturbance in the behavior of its citizens. Our government is doing heavy research with drugs and wants everyone to think the same. This mixture of drugs each has its own spirit. Painkillers and alcohol used excessively could lead to physical, emotional, and social pain and open the door to evil spirits. Marijuana has its nodding spirit. Strife is another spirit that keeps some mess going on everywhere the carrier goes with it. Strife has envy, jealousy, and every evil work coming from it.

America, it is time for you to take your medicine from the great physician. Be transformed by the renewing of your mind. Mental kidnapping is the formula for a healthy thought life that fights stress and inner debate, conflict, and disharmony. Learn how to let God fight the spiritual war in you by using his Word. Fight against alcohol, sorcery, and witchcraft and see their relationship through manipulation and what they all have in common. Fight against spiritual wickedness in high places, principalities, and powers and against generational curses. Fear is False Evidence Appearing Real or Forced Energy Against Righteousness.

Let's bless America and keep our minds strong and focused on being a better America. America, this is not a test. Mental kidnapping will keep your mind set on higher and more profitable and beneficial matters.

This book will help you get maximum results out of your life. It will make America big, better, and then best, and when the rest of the world gets better, the better in America will get best. You will become strong as you go through the storms of life while holding onto your faith and the promises as you put all your trust in God. Mental kidnapping is the remedy and will help restore you from negative words coming out of other people's mouths and of course your own.

The Word of God can help you when your brain has been fried by drugs and confused by the enemy. It will help switch your mind from wrong thinking into thinking you can. The Word will help heal your body and cleanse your mind of pollutants that can lead to family breakdowns. It will help reverse wrong thinking that comes from TV and whatever else is sending wrong signals to you. Ezekiel 18:23 (KJV) says, "Have I any pleasure at all that the wicked should die? Saith the Lord God: and not that he should return from his ways, and live?"

This book is a weapon. Use it. It will transform and renew your mind. Help change the world one mind at a time. Start reading so we can put some super on top of that natural. Optimize your life to bring out the best in you using the answer book, the Bible. Start defeating bad thoughts and madness that surrounds you.

America has chosen Barabbas and crucified Jesus Christ. America has become the Wild West. There are more people getting killed by guns than ever. There are too many walking around not operating in the Holy Spirit and not knowing the value of life. This is who I call the walking dead, yet they are alive.

CHAPTER 2

Emancipate Yourself from Mental Slavery

The Walking Dead

> Then said He unto me, Prophesy unto the wind, prophesy, son of man, and say to the wind, thus saith the Lord God; Come from the four winds, O breath and breathe upon these slain, that they may live. So, I prophesied as he commanded me, and breath came into them and they lived, and stood up upon their feet an exceeding great army. Therefore prophesy and say unto them, thus saith the Lord God; Behold O my people, I will open your graves and cause you to come up out of your graves and bring you into the land of Israel. And you shall know that I am the Lord, when I have opened your graves, And shall put my spirit in you and ye shall live, and I shall place you in your own land; then shall ye know that I the Lord have spoken it, saith the Lord. (Ezekiel 37:9–10, 12–14 KJV)

Jesus came that we might have life, and we better start living. Few people know the exact value of their lives. A man is a slave to whatever controls him. Who have you been listening to? Satan spoke to Eve, and Adam and Eve died spiritually; they became the walking dead, and when something is dead, vultures come. Jesus said Lazarus was not dead but asleep. We have to remember that the Holy Spirit will mark us present on the day of salvation from sin. Death is the completion of our lives on earth, so we should not grieve the Holy Spirit God placed in us.

We must expose the pleasures of darkness that the ungodly indulge in by letting the light of Christ shine on them. We must run to God. We should not give up on the walking dead because they are not dead but asleep. By faith, we should go to them giving them hope and wake up the healing in their bodies. We should wake up abundance and not limit God. Stay away from those who say that it won't work or that it won't happen. Obey God's Word for all your needs; the Word will work only if you work the Word. I was among the walking dead without Jesus Christ; I was lying on my back paralyzed and in a coma, left for dead. But when I got on the winning team and got closer to God, he raised me up just as he raised up Justin the Spirit. I found out that I was not alone and that Jehovah was still going ahead clearing the way for me. "Not by power nor by might but by my spirit says the Lord."

Many don't go to church because they are afraid to be seen in public places because they are criminals. Do you think a bank robber wants to be seen in a public place? No! He is one of those people who can't fully enjoy the fruit of his labor because he is always being pursued by the law. Sin makes the nonchurchgoers cowards who hide from God. They don't want to be seen in church by the people they have violated.

Some sinners go to jail for their misdeeds and find God there, but when they are released, they become the walking dead again and continue trying to be their own gods. They know about God, but they play Russian roulette with their lives, and most of the ones I see on the news get the bullet or long jail sentences. They want to come to church, but they are mentally kidnapped by guilt, shame, and condemnation—attributes of Satan. They prefer to keep on getting paid by their counterfeit jobs. They go to work, but they work to do evil. They think they are doing right, but God will judge them.

They have an excellent work ethic, but they are evil and wicked because they are employed by Satan, who offers no lasting benefits. What they do to others only boomerangs back on them. Many are living contrary to God and his Word. They talk bad about God's people just because they are afraid of coming in and being exposed and arrested. You will be surprised at why people say no when you ask them to come to church with you. They even know some people in church who commit the same sins they do, which makes coming harder. At least, those are on their way to deliverance; they are not still acting like Adam and Eve when they sinned in the garden of Eden. They are not hiding in the bushes trying to cover up their sin from God. If you have a sin sickness, you need to come in and meet the great physician, Jesus Christ.

The apostle Paul wrote to the walking dead in Ephesians 5:14: "Awake oh sleeper and rise up from the dead and Christ shall give you light." The walking dead are trying to take over our society and leading us into all wrong. Ephesians 2:1 (LB) tells us, "They actually have no clue that they are committing a sin." They know not what they do. All those who are in their sin are dead in sin. Sin is the death of the soul. Those who are spiritually dead lose their kingly or queenly status.

When we sin, our crowns fall off. When we sin, we conform to the world. We must give America and the world its medicine—Jesus Christ.

> Those who let themselves be controlled by their lower nature lives only to please themselves, but those who follow after the Holy Spirit find themselves doing those things that please God. David was a man after God's own heart. The flesh never did obey God's laws and it never will.

Pornography is nothing but an illusion that gives a person the promise of sex. This disease breaks up families and marriages and is a gateway to other illicit habits. David saw Bathsheba bathing, and he killed her husband and lost his son. The odds of divorce double for men and triple for women. We must treat every human being as our relative. There is one blood in all humans. Blacks, whites, men and women, gays and lesbians have been offended, and now God is offended by their offense. Romans 12:2 (LBT) says, "Don't copy the behavior and customs of the world but be a new and different person with a fresh newness in all you do and think."

When we walk in sin, we have thought patterns that are contrary to God and his Word. Proverbs 2:166 tells us about God's wisdom:

> It will save you from the unfaithful wife who try to lead you into adultery with her pleasing words. She leaves her husband when she was young. She ignores the promises she made before God. Death is in her house. No one who goes to her comes back or walk in the path of life again.

The ropes of sin can tie you up and mentally kidnap you and hold you captive to your foolishness. Be careful of what you think because your thoughts run your life.

We can have wrong and right thinking. Satan attacks our minds and will have us reasoning in our thinking. The right and wrong thinking brings up arguments in our minds. Right is fussing at wrong. TV news show that wrong is winning a lot of battles in people's minds. If the right thought is not what we want to do, we want to justify our wrong thoughts to give us a reason to go ahead and do what we have been doing and thinking all the time. Yes, we have debates in our minds. When we have unclean thoughts helping us make wrong choices, that brings with it an unclean spirit. When we keep cultivating these unclean thoughts, they will be the entrance point for demons. Satan works through thoughts, ideas, and suggestions. God examines the heart's deepest thoughts.

When you keep entertaining a wrong thought, your mind will become fixed on wrong thinking. We must answer wrong thoughts by renouncing, rejecting, repenting, and replacing these wrong thoughts with the Word of God. When you think about taking or stealing from others, remember, "My God shall supply all my needs according to His riches in glory by Christ Jesus." When Big Botty Suzy walk by with her revealing top, remember, "There has no temptation taken you" and look for that way out. Men, run for your life. God wants to give you his brain by giving you the mind of Christ and holding the thoughts, feelings, and purposes of his heart. Jesus told the crowd in Mark 7:14 (LB), "That their souls were not harmed by what you eat, but by what you think and say." And in vv. 20–23, he added,

It is the thought life that pollutes for from within, out of men's heart comes evil thoughts of lust, theft, murder, adultery, wanting what belongs to others, wickedness, deceit, lewdness, envy, slander, pride and all other folly. All these vile things come from within, they are what pollutes you and makes you unfit for God. You will learn from your own experiences how his ways will satisfy you.

When I listen to people talk, I hear junk conversation most of the time. Junk conversation is not profitable or productive. It doesn't build up; it talks only about someone or something. It's just something to say. Jesus said we must repent and be born again.

Have you ever asked yourself why you believe what you do and whether it's correct? It's the style for people to believe what they want to believe and reject absolute truth. They are separated from God because of the choice they made to not serve him. You are the author of your own ruin. Isaiah 50:1 says, "Man sells himself by his own sin and lust to work wickedness." God allows you to be conquered by the enemy. God made laws to identify sinners who are immoral and impure homosexuals, kidnappers, liars, those who contradict the glorious good news of our God Jehovah. Those who have wicked hearts hold onto their pain. They die young, and their lives end in disgrace.

God saves those who suffer, and if they listen through their pain, God will deliver them from their troubles and suffering. He will set a table before them in the presence of their enemies and give them the best things in life. The Prodigal Son got the best robe after he remembered his father. Mephibosheth ate at King David's table. Never think you are not worthy to eat at the king's table. When God brings you through, everyone will know he did that. God calls the thunderbolt into his hand, and when people hear it, they become silent because they know it is Jehovah God. Job 37:7 says, "God wants you to be strong like a man. But he tells the proud this is where your proud ways stop. When God placed the sea and it cannot go beyond its boundaries."

Race and gender are not your enemies. You need to wake up and snap out of it because you are your own worst enemy. How you were raised, your experiences growing up, and all your decisions make you think the way you do. Deuteronomy 30:19 tells us that God has set before you life and death, a blessing and a curse, and he said choose. What we choose comes with consequences. God's hand is stretched out still sending his Word, but sinners are mocking it. When I read God's Word, I don't see anything funny in all the killing and bloodshed before Christ. All the killing for disobedience was what held my attention. Check your hearts when the devil make you laugh not at a story but at God's Word. When you walk out the door, I hope you have your choices together. The only thing I had joy in the Word of God was, "The joy of the Lord is my strength." I was glad the devil was already defeated. Everything else was serious business. The cup of sin is already full. No matter how many laws humanity passes, God made an agreement with humanity when he created man and woman: "Be fruitful and multiply."

In the beginning, God made an agreement with day and night that they would come at the right times every day. Not even the Supreme Court can change God's agreements. If it can't change the agreement of day and night, it will not stop man and woman from being fruitful and multiplying. The Supreme Court is telling us that night is day, but we know the difference. God made the laws for the sky and the earth. What is funny about "When Jesus came to His own … His own received him not"? They knew not because they would not know the things that belong to their peace. We need to put our minds on things above and not the things of earth. We should lose our lower-life lusting in a beastly manner between one another's legs and coveting what someone else has.

"Not by power, nor by might, but by my spirit saith the Lord." God helped me get a $36,000 college loan forgiven. Lazarus was not dead but asleep. Let the Holy Spirit in you help wake up dead situations and conditions in your life. Sarah was ninety, but she believed God as did Abraham. Let's keep God out of the box. We must wake-up the dead in all things in life. "God came that we might have life and have life more abundantly."

Mental Kidnapping II

Mental kidnapping teaches you to train your mind to think on good things and to have the mind of Christ. The enemy kidnapped our minds in the garden of Eden and programmed humanity with fear, worry, doubt, and anxiety to undermine the will and plan of Jehovah. This is what I call mental slavery, and we must stay free because of its skillful and seductive arts that the enemy uses to keep us in bondage. The true knowledge of God is love, joy, peace, long-suffering, kindness, goodness, faithful, gentleness, and self-control. Technology helps us be everything but ourselves by running away from the job of perfecting ourselves through Christ Jesus. It is easier to follow the trends of today than to be our perfect selves.

Society looks more like Medusa; when it looks at itself, it hides from itself because of all its ugliness, guilt, shame, and condemnation. The world has a balm but will not apply it to the wound of its society. Jesus Christ is the healer, and he heals all. We apply everything on the wound but what heals it, and now our society looks like gangrene. We need not call it just sin; we should call the name of that spirit whatever spirit of sin it is. Cast that imagination down and send it back to the pits of hell where it belongs in Jesus's mighty name we pray.

People are being defiled by wrong associations such as television, the internet, and family members. When we defile something, we make it lose purity. Incest is a defilement. Children subject to child pornography are defiled, and that can result in uncontrolled sexual behavior. Having sexual intercourse with a person who is a virgin without consent is defilement. Bleaching the skin is a defilement of the temple of God. "Do you not know you are the temple of God and the spirit of God dwelleth in you?" (1 Corinthians 3:16). Abortion or child sacrifice and adultery are defilements. Those who think wrongly need a spiritual hospital—the church—to cure their sin sickness. Jehovah has spiritual Neosporin designed to heal all wounds, but some sinners speak against and run from the answer. They are destroyed because of their lack of knowledge that only God and the church can give. Jehovah is not looking for ability but for availability.

You will not be able to perform in heaven the sins you perform on earth. When you die and step into eternity, you will give an account of everything you did in the body. There will be no robbing, prostitution, thieves, or drug selling in hell or heaven. It will be time to receive your reward for the choices you made on earth. There will be peace in heaven and burning in hell.

Be careful to obey the Lord. Stop worshipping the way you have been with each person doing what he or she thinks is right. Beware of evil thoughts, give freely, and do not wish that you did not have to give. When you remember that Jehovah has brought you out of your Egypt, your sin, you will praise him.

Deuteronomy 18:10 (Everyday Bible) tells us, "Don't let anyone among you offer son or daughter a sacrifice in the fire (Abortion)." This is an epidemic or sin disease of fornication and adultery. Even divorce has a cure, but people walk away from the answer. Most judges tell husbands and wives to go home and work it out to keep divorce from spreading like an epidemic. That epidemic led by lesbians and women's rights advocates help diminish the thoughts of our society allied with homosexuality. On Facebook, I saw a naked man making love to a tree as if he were making love to a woman. Satan opened the door of selfishness to oppose God's plan.

Manipulation by lesbians and the women's movement has come to a head against manhood, and money is the motive. Fashion designers, men and women, are making men's clothing look like women's styles. Homosexuality is an unthoughtful designer act done by a man or woman, and it is not the original plan of God. This is a pagan act of sex orally and anally and with goats or other animals. Today, I saw a dog with human eyes. Are the eyes the window to the soul? The things that people do in darkness are unspeakable. At night, they go about thinking no one sees.

The nation's plan to defy Jehovah is collapsing; it will have to find money another way, not by accusing men with money of past manipulative acts. This was part of the plan of the enemy to manipulate the Supreme Court. Now, the Me Too movement will have to come full circle because you can't hide from yourself, and it all boils down to who you are and what you do. Has Me Too become a job?

We must always have a ready mind to have the manifestation of the Holy Spirit in us. The same venom will be the serum that heals. The kingdom is in operation in us when we remember what God has done for us. The devil was trying to take me out, but God used the venom of Satan and turned it around so I could be a serum for others. When I survived, I became a means of healing others. What the devil meant for evil, God used for my good. Don't go without the Holy Spirit in operation. Remember the seven sons of Sceva in Acts 19:1–17, and don't leave home fully armed.

Don't let anyone use magic of witchcraft or try to explain the meaning of signs (v. 11). Don't let anyone try to control others with magic or drugs, and don't let there be mediums or try to talk with spirits of the dead. The Lord hates anyone who does these things because the other nations do these things. Verse 12 reads, "But you must be innocent in the presence of the Lord." God hates magic that drugs, controls, and manipulates (witchcraft). God also warns us about the prophet that says something that he did not say though he was supposed to be speaking for him in Deuteronomy 18:22. Something the prophet said didn't come to pass. This means the prophet was speaking his own ideas. Don't be afraid of him. Let's deal with fallacies and mistaken beliefs especially those based on unsound arguments. The potential for fallacy lies behind the notion of self-esteem, the notion that cameras never lie.

God will ruin the plans of those in the streets producing trouble and tricking others. At that time, wise people think they are the only wise people, and when they die, wisdom will die with them. God uncovers the deep things of darkness. Their sin teaches their mouths what to say. Your words try to trick others, but they show you are wicked. Your lips testify against you. This is a rebellious spirit that shakes its fist at Jehovah God as it carries him or her away from God. This Jezebel rebellious spirit plans trouble and gives birth to evil whose hearts plan ways to trick others. Their minds are closed to understanding. Job 24:13–17 (Everyday Bible paraphrased) says,

> They think night is day and wrong is right and right is wrong not knowing God and His ways. They fight against the light. At night they go about like thieves thinking that no one sees them as they keep their faces covered. In the dark they break into houses and in the day, they lock the doors to their house until dark. This is because they want nothing to do with the light.

Does this sound familiar to you?

Witchcraft

> But draw near hither ye sons of the sorceress, the seed of the adulterer and whore. Against whom do ye sport yourselves? Against whom make ye a wide mouth, and draw out the tongue? Are ye not the children of transgression, a seed of falsehood.(Isaiah57:3–4KJV)

Witchcraft walks the streams among smooth stones. Witches claim to possess magical powers and practice sorcery. They are spiteful and skilled in their craft. They cause negative things to happen and bring confusion. They do this by speaking negative words toward you or someone else. They also send prayers that are words not inspired by the Holy Spirit toward you and against you. So right now, bind, rebuke, cast down, and bring to no effect all powers, principalities, evil forces, and all spiritual wickedness in the world that is coming against you and your family and those doing the work of God. Bind, rebuke, cast down, and bring to no effect all negative words coming out of people's mouths. Break and render useless all prayers not inspired by the Holy Spirit that may have been placed against you in the mighty name of Jesus Christ.

They have a witches' Sabbath that is a meeting of witching supposed by medieval Christians to be a demonic orgy. They have sex under every green tree with a magical or irresistible influence as they use their power to charm and enchant. They kill children throwing them into ravines like abortion. They charm when they induce by having a strong personal attraction that is pleasing and delightful like drugs and Satan.

Today, pornography, nude clubs, and magazines seem to cast a spell. America's television seems to be falling in love with enchantments to attract and delight their audiences' curiosity, which allows an entry for demon activity. Whatever you open your mind to can control you. Women are investing in legal power to gain authority. They are equipping, supplying, and enabling each other. People are amazed by how sorcery plays with their intelligence as it fascinates them. Children are being taught in homes evil before they can learn what is good. Learning God's ways will help bring out the greatness in them so they will be able to serve others. Adam and Eve was caught early before they had learned to reject evil and chose good.

The American Heritage College Dictionary says,

> Witchcraft is a believer and follower of Wicca, a Wiccan.
> Wicca is a polytheistic Neo Pagan nature religion inspired
> by various Christian western European beliefs whose central

deity is a mother goddess that has a Trinity Goddess of maiden the mother and then crone and which includes the use of herbal magic and benign witchcraft. The mother goddess who represents or is a personification of motherhood, fertility, creation destruction who embodies the bounty known as the Earth Mother or Mother of the Earth.

The mother in some newer forms of Wicca, such as feminist or Dianic Wicca. The Triple Goddess has been adopted are ones who argues the concept of the triple moon goddess as Maiden, Mother and Crone. Crone is an old woman who is disagreeable and malicious, sinister, a witchlike old woman.

This must be why we should love our neighbor as ourselves. Don't get on the bad side of an elderly woman.

The word crone comes from crown, indicating wisdom emanating from the head. A hag comes from hagio meaning holy. (Google Crone, hag, and witch). The crone is also known to some as a wise old woman indicating age and honor. Often having magical or super natural associations that can make her either helpful or obstructing. Obstructing means to block an opening like Satan who is a blockbuster. He blocks the opening path hinder and get in the way of your progress. He hinders your movement and try to bring you to a standstill. They deliberately make something difficult.

Wicca is given primacy or exclusivity in believers of this witchcraft. Wiccans depart from God and deal with the devil by putting a negative twist on God's Word. They worship the god of luck and have a feast to the god of fate. Jehovah God decides your fate. God wants to hold you in his arms and comfort you while bouncing you on his knee as his child. The word *witch* was said to come from wit, which means wise. Witches choose evil instead of holiness. These witches, adulterers, and sorcerers (drug dealers) are seeds of falsehood. "But she was plucked up in fury, she was cast down to the ground, and the east wind dried up her fruit: her strong rods were broken and withered; the fire consumed them" (Ezekiel 19:12 KJV).

Drug dealers live only to satisfy their own stomachs. They carry sin around in their pockets and women in their breasts like the sorcerers and sorceresses of the ancient days. The purpose of this magical trick is to bring negative effects on the user's pocket to make a positive one on theirs. The user is at the mercy of the dealer, who thinks he is a doctor and chemist who knows how to prepare drugs. The pharmacist has the real thing while the streets put together anything they can to make it look close to the real thing. There are so many it is an epidemic in our society that has spread and can be fatal like AIDS.

Everything God made is good, but the devil has a counterfeit for it. Satan cannot create; he can only try to duplicate or destroy what God has already created. In the late sixties and early seventies, people were selling hallucinating drugs called orange sunshine, purple haze, and window pain. These drugs were used by the gang members of the seventies called motorcycle clubs. This was the same spirit that you see in today's society with people sporting tattoos, the "I'm free to do whatever I want with my body" crowd. In the late sixties and early seventies, these group were outcasts like homosexuals. Today, this rebellious spirit influences society. This spirit of rebellion needs to be cast out of this generation.

During the hippie movement, people took drugs and tripped out. Today, everyone rebels against God's laws. Different drug, different time, but the same spirit. My experience was that it was better to go on the trip with someone you know because no one else knew what you were going through. The drugs they sold were only a figment of the buyer's imagination. It kept them chasing a feeling they would never obtain again.

It took them into a world of confusion and corruption where everything they did became a curse.

The drugs of sorcerers and witches can also cause hallucinations that lead to social, physical, and emotional harm. We need to foster social awareness if we want social wellness in our communities.

> For we wrestle not against flesh and blood, but against principalities, against powers, against the rulers of darkness

of this world, against spiritual wickedness in high places.
Wherefore take unto you the whole armour of God, that
ye may be able to withstand in the evil day, and done all
to stand.

Read the next verse in your Bible until you have your whole armor
on. Pray God's Word, and always remember that every word you
speak is a continual prayer. "Life and death are in the power of the
tongue." The Holy Spirit told me that there was no such thing as a
junk conversation. Keep God's Word first place, active, and on the
scene.

Isaiah 57:4 reads, "They are children of transgression or children
of disobedience. The prophet says to them come and I will read you
your doom." This is a generation of scoffers and scorners. They bad-
mouth God, his prophets whose message they deliver, and the church.

The Jezebel spirit called witchcraft is controlling and rebellious.
Galatians 3:1 (LB) reads, "O foolish Galatians What magician has
hypnotized you and cast an evil spell upon you?" This spirit of
intimidation, manipulation, and domination is out in full force.
Jezebel is a spirit that destroys life, a seducing spirit that will entice
and attract you into the wrong spiritual activity. This spirit rejects
the authority of God and the leaders God put in authority to give us
guidance.

This controlling spirit is found in men and women. People will
try to rule and run your life if you let them. In Genesis, you see how
Joseph's brothers turned his life upside down, but the Lord was with
him. David was a shepherd, and his father brought everybody in the
room to be anointed king but him. But the Lord was with David.
I thank God for being in me, on me, around me, and for me. In 1
Kings 14:24, we read about how King Ahab promoted prostitution
all over his kingdom. It was cult prostitution; effeminate men who
were sodomites sold their bodies. This was a condition that God went
before the Israelites to clear out of their way so they would not be
contaminated. God wanted Israel to be free of witchcraft just as he
wants his people today to be free from witchcraft. To deal with this
spirit, you must recognize it and confront it with the kingdom of God,
the gospel of Christ, and the blood of Jesus that covers you. Confront

it face to face advising deliverance to that spirit in that person to what the spirit of God says: "Greater is he that is in me than he who is in the world." Bring the light in you to dark places, to those using their love potions that create sexual desires and curses. Those who speak negative words are not inspired by the Holy Spirit. They deal in fortune- telling and divination. They intimidate others with their money and forceful personalities. They manipulate others in skillful, unscrupulous, and clever ways. They take authority where they are not authorized to override others' decisions. They force their will on others. We must stay in the secret place dwelling in the Word of God and abide under the shadow of the Almighty. We must commune with God and his Word by reading and meditating on it and praising and praying to God. We must agree with Jehovah by speaking his Word. He is our refuge and our fortress in whom we put our trust. We should always remind ourselves that we are covered in the blood of Jesus Christ.

You don't have to engage in fortune-telling and divination because God already has a plan for your life; he knows the end from the beginning. The devil shows you the beginning but never the end. The network of Jezebel has only chains of bondage, traps, snares, death, and destruction. Just like the story of Balaam and Balak, they want to send curses against Israel. It will be nothing but stepping stones and blessings for God's people. When we are saved and become one with Jesus Christ, we cannot be cursed because no one can curse whom Jehovah God has blessed. Nothing but sin can separate us from the love of God. We must consecrate ourselves and wash ourselves with the Word of God to make ourselves clean in his sight. If you are practicing witchcraft, that might be the reason death and destruction are going on in your family. Jezebel manipulated her whole family into death with that whorish, rebellious spirit. Remember that rebellion is as bad as sin and witchcraft. You must not try to tell the future by signs and black magic. In Leviticus 19:26 (Everyday Bible), God said,

"I will be against anyone who goes to a mediums and fortune tellers for advice, because that person is being unfaithful to me."

"As the bird by wandering and as the swallow by flying so the curse causeless shall not come." Speak the Word of God over the situation and make the curse that was spoken over you have no effect.

Do not be in sin and give it a cause to open for the curse. The negative words spoken to Christians will just bounce off them and return to the sender. "Let destruction come upon him unawares; and let the net that he has hidden catch himself: into that very destruction let him fall and my soul shall be joyful in the Lord" (Psalm 35:8).

"Delight thyself in the Lord; and he shall give thee the desires of your heart" (Psalm 37:4). "Just seek ye first his kingdom his righteousness his way of doing and being right and all these other things will be added unto you." Witches use alcohol and drugs as their tools to make you weak while they study you to see how it affects you to have power over you.

Sex is also a tool of witches and has become a sport and a business. The idea of having sex to have a baby is obsolete today. Some women's sex organs are becoming graveyards because of abortions. They seem not to show any remorse or even have a conflict of spirit when they kill a child. Isaiah 57 says it is like throwing a child into a ravine. They have one mindset—me, me, me, me, me. Some women have gone back to using the knowledge of ancient woman to claim their place in a male-dominated society. They have gone back to use the knowledge of the witch crone called women's liberation. Some woman and men will choose evil, but most will choose holiness. God said, "Be ye Holy for I am Holy," and he knows your sacrifice and suffering.

People are always looking for ways to predict the future. No one can help another person see what will happen in the future (Ecclesiastes 3:22). Daniel interpreted Nebuchadnezzar's dream through the will of God telling him that iron and clay did not hold together. The people of America are not holding together. The United States has a mixture of races but does not honor Jehovah, who has power over their lives and everything they do. They want to add to what God has done. Just look and see how silly man and woman are becoming without Christ trying to add to what God has already done and made them to be. Ecclesiastes 3:14 (Everyday Bible) says, "I know that everything God does will continue forever." People cannot add anything to what God has done, and they can't take anything away from it. What is happening now has happened in the past.

In the first chapter of Esther, a queen named Vashti was trying to get women to rebel against their husbands. The way she acted did not honor their husbands. It's all about agreement, not division; a house divided cannot stand. Man and woman were put here to rule together, but Queen Vashti started to hang out with the women's lib crowd, and she became defiled and polluted with unnecessary debates. That threw a monkey wrench into her marriage. She was a queen and did not need anything. The only thing she was not was king or God, but she was a god to her rebellious followers.

That was a satanic move just as Lucifer's pride made him want to be God. Vashti and Satan were kicked out of their kingdoms because of pride. Satan felt empowered just as women today feel empowered, filled with pride. Warning comes before destruction, and a haughty spirit comes before a fall. Where and what will the fall be? What is so honorable about constant disrespect and anger? You are either together or not. Each man is still ruler over his family. Their disrespect toward God brings curses on the family because no one is covered. No man or woman wants to bury a son or daughter. No man or woman wants to admit that a son or daughter is someone the world could do without. Charity starts at home. This silly woman Vashti did not even want to put her crown on to rule an enormous kingdom; she wanted just to argue. Nothing else to do but hang out with thugs—the hardheaded, rebellious, disrespectful, and disobedient crowd. I called her silly because in 2 Timothy 3:6, Paul spoke of the stealthy way such women worm their way into homes where weak women with consciences burdened with sin are ready prey for those who promise ease of conscience if they will but follow their erroneous teaching. As these women lived in a state of comparative exclusion, fraud and deceit were necessary for the false teachers to enter their apartments. Paul described these women whose good home lives were often disrupted by crafty teachers as silly, lacking sense, stupid, weak in the mind, and spiritually immature. They were Christian in name only; they were impulsive and emotional and lacked depth of character and became easy prey for lying doctrine and false peace offered by those who had a form of godliness but who were destitute of its power. Christian women in the church in Ephesus and the church today need to constantly pray for spiritual intuition to enable them to turn immediately from alien voices to the clear Word. It was like the song from the Temptations, "It was just my imagination once again running away with me."

Prayer of Forgiveness

Heavenly Father, in the name of Jesus Christ, I let go of all bitterness, resentment, envy, strife, and unkindness. I give no place to the devil. I ask you to forgive and release all who have wronged and hurt me. I forgive and release them in Jesus's name. By faith, I receive your forgiveness having assurance that I am cleansed of all unrighteousness through Jesus Christ. If you forgive others their trespasses, your heavenly Father will forgive you, but if you do not forgive others' trespasses, your heavenly Father will not for give your trespasses.

Barabbas: Murderous Spirit

The world has released Barabbas and crucified Jesus Christ. There is a murderous spirit in our midst. Sing a funeral song for the United States. God wants to make your beauty perfect so you will not come to a terrible end. While you are having your terrible end, you will want to think you are your own god. Satan was ruined by his pride and was cast down from heaven. Sin has given us horror, amazement, and contempt. Murder induced by drugs, alcohol, and anger is running rampant in our society.

Everything we do begins with a thought. We must stand up as we really are. We should not be hanging with people who measure themselves by themselves or those who do not honor or obey God's Word. Wherever we stand in America seems like a graveyard, and we all will lie down in death. Graves have been made for us with those we think we are better than in our pride, even those who have done us wrong.

The righteous perish because bullets shot by those who are angry don't have eyes. God removes them from the danger to come. "The happiness of the righteous is their removal." Evil men and those who are full of pride lie in their beds plotting how to gain by fraud and violence. Micah 2:3 (LB) reads, "But the Lord says, I will reward your evil with evil; nothing can stop me; never again will you be proud and haughty after I am through with you." God is talking to those who want to be their own gods and have murder on their hearts and tongues. They fight the answer. Evil will destroy the wicked.

When evil people are not punished right away, it make others want to do evil. I watched news about a man who robbed an old woman and stole her car; he drove away but died in a traffic accident. He reaped what he sowed. Burglars break into people's homes and are shot and killed. These people plot their own deaths. Ezekiel 35:6 (Everyday Bible) says, "Since you like murder, murder will pursue you." The King James Version puts it this way: "Therefore, as I live, saith the Lord God, I will prepare thee unto blood, and blood shall pursue thee: sith thou hast not hated blood, even blood shall pursue thee." They forgot that they are a puff of smoke here just for a moment and then they die. If this is you, know that God is not mad at you; instead, Jehovah is mad about you. God doesn't like talking to you so roughly; he is just threatening you for your own good and wants to put you on the right path. God hates sin.

Parents and the government ought to know right from wrong but hate good and love evil; they are doing right wrong. Our leaders are passing laws to make us believe day is night and night is day. Do you like anyone playing with your mind? This is not a test. They spit in our hands and tell us it's raining.

I let heaven fill my thoughts with Christ's mighty energy working in me. In him lies hidden all the mighty untapped treasures of wisdom and knowledge. In Christ, we have all of God in us. I am living in the spirit world and am letting go the things of the flesh so I can fight my real enemy, the one I can't see. Guns are flooding our neighborhoods, and gun stores are becoming targets for thieves. In some states, it is legal to have guns in cars and parks. Seems like everybody is getting an update on artillery. There are some real moves being made in America when it comes to the distribution of guns.

God breathed life into our bodies, and we have souls. My homeland is in heaven, the origin of life as the Bible explains. God is spirit, and those who worship him must worship him in spirit and in truth. The breath we breathe is from God. Jesus is my friend because he is the words I speak from the scriptures. God is my Father; he wants our honor. The Holy Spirit is my guidance counselor. We work together as a team against the enemy. All those who have devil-inspired ideas tell lies with straight faces. God wants us to have clean thoughts. We need to run from evil thoughts. When I got tired of sinning and came to my senses, I began to escape Satan'strapsandsnares.

The enemy was working through people close to me, and I was wondering why I kept falling. When I let my guard down from doing God's Word with the ones showing their wickedness, I always would end up worse than before. I had to find out it was not that person but the spirit dwelling in that person. I was certain that the person was trying to take me out because every time I sinned around that person, the spirit inside that person would attack me. That same spirit followed me wherever I went. It would do the same thing in the same way with different people, but the same spirit was always trying to take me out. It happened every time when I let my guard down. Once I realized that, I begin to get back into the Word and began to get closer to God and under his protection. If you want to find me, I'll be in the secret place. Psalm 91:1 says, "He that dwelleth in the secret place of the Highest shall abide under the shadow of the Almighty."

Sorcery: Manipulating Spirits

Sorcery is mind control; a magic that exit in every culture and language and communication about reality. Anyone can fool you if you let them. We must always stay conscience. We must do this by using the power of consciousness to understand reality in greater depts of clarity. To understand logical fallacies that are tricks and illusion of thought, and cognitive biases that prevent us from understanding the manipulative techniques and mind control used against us.

This is so we will be able to have power against sorcery. Sorcery is a direction of energy manifesting in an ability or power to influence others. It is an art of using our wills to influence others for positive and negative goals, objectives, and outcomes. I hung out with sorcerers for many years never realizing they were sorcerers. We used to hustle every day to make money. It was funny because they thought they were using me and I thought I was using them. They wanted the title of boss, but all I wanted was a chance to make money. We looked at things from different perspectives. Their backgrounds were pure street, and I was in a backslidden state. I still recognized God and commanded my day, but when I went home after being a person like a used car dealer, I fell on my knees to repent. The question was who was zooming whom.

Sorcerers use their knowledge of reality to gain power over others as a negative form of magic.

> Magic is achieved through the power and ability of understanding reality. Language, Symbolism, and imagery is the tool of magicians. The greater the understanding of language, symbols, and consciousness the more power the magic is to affect the people's consciousness. It becomes "dark" as sorcery.
>
> Sorcerer's take their accurate understanding of reality and perverts it to manipulate others to their own. We buy into the product others are selling; words are spells. They are spells through spelling. Ideas are sold like a product to the consciousness of people who buy into them.
>
> The ultimate tyranny in a society is not control by martial law. It is control by phycological manipulation of consciousness through which reality is defined. So that those who exist within it do not even realize that they are in a prison. They do not realize that there is something outside of where they exist. (Bringers of the Dawn)
>
> We fool ourselves all though the power or consciousness without us agreeing to the idea of an eternalized authority over our lives. These beliefs have no power. We give them power. We except an imagined eternalized authority over our lives.

Jehovah is my authority. We need to plead guilty and make the necessary changes. We need to listen now! It is the thought life that pollutes; all vile things come from within. Another version says, "Listen, and take this to heart It is not what you swallow that pollutes your life but what you vomit up" (Matthew 15:11 Gateway).

The enemy's plots and plans have become easy to recognize with money and the television. Average Americans believe anything they see on TV. Satan is saying, "Let me control the airwaves and I can control the world." Things on television become reality for many people. Satan tries to change the world to make it like what's on TV. Money is another way the enemy manipulates our society because times get hard and men start robbing and stealing to get it. Women start selling their precious bodies to make money; the price of Jezebel products goes up. In the world, the magic words are, "How much do you like me?" and "Where's mine?"

Carjackers will chauffeur around their victims at the point of a gun. Guns are no better than those who pull the trigger. Guns cannot control those who pick them up. Guns allow people to kill their own people. Gangs in America don't even realize we are all on the same team as they Bogart their way through life living and dying fast. They trust only in money, not God, who created it.

When you find God, you have a peace that surpasses all understanding. Subliminal suggestions occur when messages or ideas that are perceived below the conscious level influence our thoughts, feelings, and actions. If you are on fire for God, you will desire to please him. Sometimes, I got cocky and decided I knew enough scriptures and stopped tending to the Word. Then when I got weak, Satan came along and asked me if I could turn a stone into bread. I had one foot in sin because I had not been nurturing the Word.

One day when I was out witnessing, Satan asked me if I could turn sinners into saints, and I said no, but God in me could. He was trying to put doubt in my heart. I prayed in the Spirit and pumped up that most Holy Spirit in me. I knew the Archangel Michael would fight for me (Daniel 12 LB). Hosea 4:1 (LB) says,

> The Lord has filed a law suit, you exchange the glory of God for the disgrace. Wine, women and song has robbed my people of their brains. There is no faithfulness, kindness, or knowledge of God in your land. You swear and lie and kill and steal and commit adultery. There is violence everywhere, with one murder after another.

Hosea 4:3 reads, "They exchanged the glory for God for idols." Verse 14 of chapter 4 reads, "There your daughters turn to prostitutes and your brides commit adultery. God said, but why should I punish them? For you men are doing the same thing, sinning with harlots and temple prostitutes. Fools your doom is sealed for you refuse to understand." Hosea 4:18 reads, "The men of Israel finish up their drinking bouts, and off they go to find some whores, their love for shame is greater than for honor." Those words put me in check, and I heard them twice the first time because I didn't want to end up in the valley of judgment.

Those who persevere in righteousness will have peace in the end. John 17:17 says, "Sanctify them through thy truth thy word is truth." Our words are no more than opinions. The Bible is the inspired Word of God. In our more advanced society, people refuse to submit to their creator and to accept his Word as truth. A wise man once said, "Those who stand for nothing will fall for anything." We all have choices that God gave us, but consequences go with the choices we make. God gave us his Word to keep us from self-destructing.

People have become very selfish, and marriages are falling apart. When families fall apart, there goes the neighborhood, the city, and the nation. Illegal drugs are causing huge problems in our country. Drug dealers push sin and death along with drugs. They are pushing immorality through TV and the internet. We don't have as much time on earth as we think, so we must hurry and get it right. One man made plans last night for this morning, but he died in his sleep. Another man made plans for this evening, but he died this afternoon. We don't know what is around the next corner of our lives.

We must replace our natural and carnal thoughts with the thoughts of God. Blacks, gays, lesbians, and women are not at hand, but the kingdom of God is at hand. Our leaders are supposed to be telling us right and wrong, yet they are the ones who are doing wrong. They are doing right wrong. They seem to hate good and love evil. Mr. Treadwell, there you go bashing again. The only bashing I'm doing is Satan bashing.

God is standing poised against our pride. Few people realize that there is a spirit influencing our world; the Bible calls it the god of this age. "In whom the god of this world hath blinded the minds of them which believe not, lest the light of the glorious gospel of Christ, who is the image of God, should shine unto them" (2 Corinthians 4:4).

All born-again believers are the image of God because of the Holy Spirit in them. The unsaved do not have the Spirit of God. They procrastinate like Pharaoh did when he was asked when he wanted the frogs removed; he said tomorrow. Tomorrow never comes because it is always a day away. We don't have time for procrastination, and I am not spending one more day with the frogs. The time is now! Today is the day the Lord has made. Today is the day for salvation. David chose five smooth stones in case Goliath had some brothers, and he put one stone, the Word, in Goliath's forehead. It's time for us to get real with ourselves and say enough is enough. Pain is a servant that lets us know something is wrong. This is a spiritual battle, and the enemy attacks our minds first. We must hold on to the Word of God or we will be defeated. Faith walks through all things that confront us. To change our environment, we must change our company. This thing is not about Nino Brown or about Steven Treadwell or about you. It is about our souls. One souls in heaven are worth all the silver and gold on earth. All races of the earth need to know Jesus. We need to teach the drug dealers, sorcerers, prostitutes, and witches that the snake on Moses's brass pole on any doctor's shoulder was meant for healing. Some people will not wait on God; they make easy money and step in front of the knowledge of God. "But we have this treasure in earthen vessels, that the excellency of the power may be of God and not of us" (2 Corinthians 4:7). Jesus quickens those who are dead in sin.

> Wherein in time past ye walked according to the course of this world, according to the prince of the power of the air, the spirit that now worketh in the children of disobedience: Among whom also we all had our conversation in times past in the lust of our flesh, fulfilling the desires of the flesh and of the mind and we were by nature the children of wrath, even as others. "But God who is rich in mercy, for his great love wherewith he loved us. (Ephesians 2:1–4)

This was done so that all could be saved and come to repentance.

Feminism: The Door to Lesbianism

Feminism is the advocacy of women's rights based on equality of the sexes. The cup of sin is full, and it will bring on only the wrath of God. God ordained man and woman to be fruitful and multiply and replenish the earth together. Now we have another group to go into the world and teach the gospel of Christ. Right! Either you are together or you are not. Now, a distraction has popped up over who got the most. We are not taking anything with us when we die, so why worry? What about the souls of men and women? Life is too short. Man and woman had the glory of God on them in the garden of Eden. God put man asleep to bring the woman into the world. Now, it seems man has been put to sleep again. We all go through difficulties. Eve ate the forbidden fruit and gave her husband some.

Feminists tear down their homes just to prove a point. They want to prove they can do whatever they want in marriage. Whatever happened to together? Feminists fall in love with each other's hurt and pain. They are children of Belial, the fallen angel that rebelled against Jehovah and was kicked out of heaven with Satan by the Archangel Michael like a lightning bolt. They personify wickedness and ungodliness. They got hurt and vowed to never have relationships with man, only with women. This open rebellion against God is putting the earth out of balance because women think they are not equal with men. They want more than equality; they want all the money and have women, who were made for men. People who break God's laws find themselves in more misery than the misery they were trying to escape. This misery comes from wrong choices that make them end up in mental prisons or drugs (Isaiah 59:5–6 Everyday Bible).

A transition in our society is occurring from God's plan into a selfish plan, what feminists think our lives should be. They think their way into transformation by renewing their minds into a male thought-life. These thoughts become a stronghold in their minds and a curse that needs to be broken in Jesus's name. They want to jump into a man's way of thinking and have not learned how to be the best women they can be. They have abandoned their posts. They should become the best women they can be and raise their children properly.

God created humanity but not feminism. Feminism is only another tactic of Satan to destroy the family that God ordained. The Word of God has healing for feminism. Kicking men out the house to show who is boss and prostituting daughters is a new way of showing a woman's independence. The Bible tells women not to prostitute their daughters. This is what you see as women go through the process of becoming equal. Feminism is the door that opens to lesbianism. Pain will make you bitter or better. There is a need to have someone to go through the pain with. Misery loves company. There is a message behind the pain we all go through. You never know what a person is going through. If you don't have on the armor of God, it will be hard to function in that pain. God forgave our sin for his sake (Isaiah 43:25). I think lesbians are bitter women who have been hurt by men and pledge never to go back into relationships with men.

I love to hear them talk about commitment to each other. They say they will never go back, but I prophesy they will all go back. What they have with each other is just another relationship. In relationships, people lie, cheat, and try to get over on one another. They still end up breaking up. From my experience, I can't see how I end up in the bed with them. They have a strong love for money so they can keep to themselves. This was something the man was to be doing. They still attract men, and money helps their relationships. They were tired of being lied to by men but are now being lied to by women because they both are living a lie. They don't want to face their relationship with Jehovah God.

God loves you and so does man because you were meant to be his rib made from man for man. We love you, and there is nothing you can do about it. As far as man was concerned, you could have always opened your own car doors, but man was only honoring and appreciating you. When I speak to two ladies in a relationship, there is one who always speaks; the other acts as though she is asking, *Why are you speaking to my woman?* There is a problem here that is not going to be in heaven. Revelation 14:13

says that blessed is the man who dies in the Lord. I just might turn that around and say cursed is the man or woman who dies outside the Lord.

Slaves to Sin

The hand of the Lord was upon me and carried me out in the Spirit of the Lord and set me down during the valley full of bones. The US has become the valley of dry bones. The street hustle was not put together for people to make a living at it. The street hustle was meant for you to hit it and quit it. They let their demons take over, and they become slaves to whatever sins they commit daily. Why would you want to make yourself a slave to any sin and die or go to jail? The street hustle was manifested by Satan so hardheaded, rebellious, lazy, bloodsucking people could make enough money to catch up and get legitimate businesses.

The hustlers are killing their neighborhoods, mothers and fathers, and sisters and brothers because of their lazy mentality. Their daydreaming is slowing America down. Can't you see that you're not getting anywhere? Get caught and give the system its cut. When you are in sin, you are a slave to sin. If you commit the same crime every day, Murphy's law will catch up with you. What can go wrong will go wrong. You are just a sitting duck. You are sticking out like a sore thumb. You are an accident just waiting to happen. When you get caught, you have just donated yourself to society. You have become a modern slave who donated your mind, body, and soul to the government.

A demon controls such toxic thinking, and it needs to be cast out. You are being pimped on by the system that you are trying to beat. You are in a merry-go-round of hopelessness. You look like the biggest tricks in America paying bail bondsmen and court costs. You should not bow to the god of this age, a fallen angel. Misery loves company and he wants you to fall with him.

John 12:31 says, "Now is the judgment of this world: Now shall the prince of this world be cast out." Why don't you wake up and stop spreading fornication and drugs just so you can have a happy meal? Let the Word of God be your happy meal. The job you have in the streets comes only to steal, kill, and destroy. The only thing you will accomplish is your death and destruction, and you know that. You know the ones who died during the process of your trying to come up the wrong way. You want work a nine-to-five job. Yeah, you know where the bodies are buried because of your ignorance and selfishness.

You will want to say John 14:30: "Hear after I will not talk much with you: for the prince in this world cometh, and hath nothing in me." It's not about power, money, fortune, or fame; it's about Jesus Christ, the keeper of our souls, and your soul know that. Jesus said it was about judgment in John 16:11: "Of judgment because the prince of this world is judged." Jesus Christ is the keeper of our souls, minds, wills, and emotions. Some people did not have any home training and hooked up with the god of this age who only came to steal, kill, and destroy, and that's the cause of the earth's trouble.

When men and women walk contrary to God, they are hooked up with a curse that makes them a curse. Everything they encounter is destroyed. They become agents of the devil. I beg NBC, ABC, and

CBS to make commercials to show you exactly what the other side of immorality and danger looks like from a spiritual point of view. In 2 Kings 9:22 (Everyday Bible), we read, "Jehu answered There will never be any order as long as your mother Jezebel worship Idols and uses witchcraft." She was a cursed woman. Yes, we as humans have choices; we're willing participants in the immoral choices we make. We try to self-destruct being used by the devil. Oops! The devil made me do it! This goes along with the choices we make. Don't give him credit though he is the one orchestrating the course our world is going in.

He is not more powerful than God. God allows and permits his rule. The couple in the garden of Eden gave the devil the authority. God gave them choices in the garden of Eden, and now we still have to choose what God said we should do or not do. God lets the enemy test and try us. Lucifer developed an exaggerated opinion of his importance. Isaiah 14:12 reads, "How art thou fallen from heaven, O Lucifer, son of the morning! How art thou cut down to the ground, which didst weaken the nations!" Lucifer served at the very throne of God. Ezekiel 28:14 (KJV) reads, "Thou art the anointed cherub that covereth; and I have set thee so: thou wast upon the holy mountain of God; thou hast walked up and down in the midst of the stones of fire."

God warns us that the devil and his angels have deceived the whole world in Revelation 12:9. Are we being deceived? Are we being mentally kidnapped? Why do we believe what we believe? Who have we been listening to? Are our friends' ideas about God true? Is every religion equal in the mind of God? Do we believe what is popular? Can we prove what we believe? We must not be deceived. The enemy is a powerful and dangerous liar.

In 1 John 2:18–19 (KJV), we read,

> Little children, it is the last time: and as ye have heard that antichrist shall come, even now are there many antichrists; whereby we know that it is the last time. They went out from us, but they were not of us for if they had been of us, they would no doubt have continued with us, but they went out, that they might be made (manifest) that they were not all of us.

They had no real loyalty to God's kingdom. Many of them don't have consciences, but Jesus came to make our consciences clear.

Jesus Christ is no doubt the greatest salesman ever. He came that we may have life and have it more abundantly. Greater than all the Trump Towers. Jesus Christ is our trump card because every time we bring him on the scene, we win. America needs to take back the airways and the internet by doing the Great Commission. "The earth is the Lord's and the fullness thereof." We must take back the airwaves before it is too late and change what we see and hear.

Remember, it is not about us—our race or sex—but about Jesus Christ. When we let race and sex dictate to us, we are being divided as a nation by the god of this age. The devil tries to divide and conquer. Even the worst sinners in the world have hope through Jesus Christ, who became man, died, and rose to let us know death no longer had dominion over us. Jesus has dominion in heaven and earth and now under the earth, hell. Some people think that God is the God only of their race, but they have the Word twisted. Christ died for all humankind.

Jesus Christ is our faith toward God, who has an abundance of mercy for humankind. Jesus came to reconcile us with God. He suffered temptation just as we do to show us we could overcome temptation and sin. Jesus came to give us all the support we need when we are tempted.

Temptations are dangerous; if we give in to them, some of them can take us out. God always gives us a way out; 1 Corinthians 10:13 says, "There hath no temptation taken you, but such is common to man: but God is faithful, who will not suffer you to be tempted above ye are able; but will with the temptation also make a way of escape, that ye may be able to bear it." Temptations are all around us. We need the Word of God written not on our bodies like tattoos but on our hearts.

When we are tempted with sin, there is always a way to escape. James 1:13–15 tells us,

> Let no man say when he is tempted, I am tempted of God: for God cannot be tempted with evil, neither tempted he any man: The Process is, But every man is tempted, when he is drawn away of his own lust, and enticed. Then when lust has conceived, it bringeth forth sin: and sin when it is finished bringeth forth death.

We have a way out of temptation if we don't conceive the lust of sin that comes into our hearts. We must resist before we are enticed.

When others deliberately irritate us, we must exercise our senses: "Therefore leaving the principles of the doctrine of Christ, let us go on to perfection; not laying again the foundation of repentance from dead works and of faith toward God" (Hebrews 6:1). Can we be right wrong? It may be in our right, but it may not be the best thing for us. God gave us all a choice, but that choice can make us have a negative impact on ourselves. We even have laws helping us make bad decisions. When the law says you can, that makes it easier because we'll consider it our right. God also gave us consciences, but some with hard hearts don't have consciences.

Many people don't seem to have consciences; they are all for self. The law is making wrong right and right wrong. When we ask Jesus to be our helper and guide, we must change how we speak, understand, and think. "We can do nothing against the truth, but for the truth." God is spirit, and those who worship him must worship him in spirit and truth. The Bible says whosoever shall call on the name of the Old (Jesus) shall be saved.

In 2 Corinthians 13:5 (KJV), we read,

> Examine yourselves, whether ye be in the faith; prove your own selves. Know ye not your own selves, how that Jesus Christ is in you, except ye be reprobate. While we look not at things which are seen, but at the things which are not seen: for the things which are seen are temporal; but the things which are not seen are eternal.

God told us to preach the Word to everyone, not just white or black people. "For God so loved the world that he gave his only begotten Son that whosoever believeth in him shall not perish but have everlasting life," and you are that whosoever.

The Egyptians had the children of Israel in slavery with black-on-black crime. I just stopped looking at someone's color and started focusing on his or her heart.

Then Peter opened his mouth and said, of a truth I perceive that God is no respecter of persons: But in every nation he that feareth him, and worketh righteousness is accepted with him. (Acts 10:34–35 KJV)

Romans 2:11 (KJV) says, "For there is no respecter of persons with God." Romans 2:28–29 (KJV) states, "For he is not a Jew which is one outwardly; neither is that circumcision, which is outward in the flesh: But he is a Jew, which is one inwardly; and circumcision is that of the heart, in the spirit, and not in the letter; whose praise is not of men, but of God." The law was that all males in your house, even slaves, had to be circumcised. Abraham was the father of faith, and I am of the blessings of Abraham. Galatians 3:28–29 (KJV) reads, "There is neither Jew nor Greek, there is neither bond nor free, there is neither male nor female: for ye are all one in Christ Jesus. And if ye be Christ's, then are ye Abraham's seed, and heirs according to the promise." When the world sees the saints being blessed, they want to rub shoulders with them as though they have the same spirit, but they are of the flesh with just a little more grace. They have a sin and slavery mentality while the saints have an "I am not bound in sin" mentality because they are covered by the blood of Jesus Christ. Whom the Son sets free is free indeed. Once you free your mind, your butt will follow.

Galatians 4:29–31 (KJV) says,

But as then he that was born after the flesh persecuted him that was born after the Spirit, even so it is now. Nevertheless what saith the scriptures? Cast out the bondwoman and her son: for the son of the bondwoman shall not be heir with the son of the freewoman. So then, brethren, we are not children of the bondwoman, but of the free.
For through him we both have access by one Spirit unto the Father. (Ephesians 2:18 KJV)

The world will not access the Spirit of God though it is available to them. We should not let the child of the bondwoman stop us from our God-ordained destiny. We should be all in the same spirit of God.

"In whom ye also are builder together for a habitation of God through the Spirit" (Ephesians 2:22 KJV). When we are saved, the Spirit of God is in us no matter what race or gender we are. We are a house of God through the Spirit. God took away the Old Testament so he could establish the New Testament by putting his Spirit in us.

Hebrews 10:7, 9 (KJV) reads,

> Then said I, Lo, I come in the volume of the book: It is written of me, to do thy will, O God." Then said he, Lo, I come to do thy will, O God, He taketh away the first that he may establish the second.
> There is a spirit of Truth and a spirit of error. The spirit of error will lead you the wrong way and It will keep you from wanting to hear the truth.

In 2 Corinthians 4:5–7, we read,

> For we preach not our ourselves, but Christ Jesus the Lord; and ourselves your servant for Jesus sake. For God who commanded the light to shine out of darkness hath shined in our hearts, to give the light of the knowledge of the glory of God in the face of Jesus Christ. But we have this treasure in earthen vessels that the excellencies of the power may be of God and not of us.

That power is for everyone. (I suggest you read all of Romans 5). "Therefore, being justified by faith we have peace with God through our Lord Jesus Christ: By whom also we have access by faith into the grace wherein we stand and rejoice in hope of the glory of God" (Romans 5:1–2). "If so, be that ye have heard him, and have been taught by him, as the truth is in Jesus" (Ephesians 4:21 KJV). Remember that truth is the supreme reality, the ultimate meaning and value of existence. John 17:17 (KJV) says, "Sanctify them through thy truth thy word is truth" So if you are gay, lesbians, Klan, Hebrew—whatever—check yourself before you wreck yourself about the Spirit in you and keep color and your limited imagination out of God's Word.

Read Romans verses 22–32 and you will be able to fix your mouth toward what to believe.

> Jesus Christ is God and God is Spirit and those who worship must worship Him in spirit and in truth. See now that I, even I am he, and there is no god with me (Deuteronomy 32:39)
>
> For we must all appear before the judgment seat of Christ; that everyone may receive the things done in his body, according to that he has done, whether it be good or bad. And that he died for all, that they which live should not henceforth live unto themselves, but unto him which died for them, and rose again. (2 Corinthians 5:10, 15)
>
> I speak not this to condemn you: for I have said before, that ye are in our hearts to die and live with you. (2 Corinthians 7:3)
>
> For we commend not ourselves again unto you, but give you occasion to glory on our behalf, that ye may have somewhat to answer them which glory in appearance and not in heart. (2 Corinthians 5:12)
>
> Do you look on the things on the outward appearance? If any man trust to himself that he is Christ's, let him of himself think this again, that as he is Christ even so are we Christ" For we dare not make ourselves of the number, or compare ourselves with some that commend themselves, but they measure themselves by themselves, and comparing themselves among themselves, are not wise. (2 Corinthians 10:12)

Many sit in barber shops and beauty salons and compare themselves to others. In 2 Corinthians 11:3–4, we read,

> But I fear lest by any means, as the serpent beguiled Eve through his subtlety, so your minds should be corrupted from the simplicity that is in Christ . For if he that cometh preaching another Jesus whom we have not preached, or if ye receive another spirit, which ye have not received, or another gospel which ye have not accepted, ye might well bear with him.

Are they Hebrews? So am I. Are they Israelites? So am I. Are they the seed of Abraham? So am I. Sometimes in our journey, we run into false brethren, and debate, envy, wrath, strife, backbiting, whispering, and other evils result. Jesus will come back and find us still in sin.

We should fear God and keep his commandments because mental kidnapping goes on in these places. We must keep God's Word and man's laws. "God is not a man that he should lie neither the son of man that he should repent." We must keep God's commandments so he will make us win in every area in our lives. God first wants us to be born again.

CHAPTER 3

Emancipate Yourself from Mental Slavery

Being born again? This is a term I've heard all my Christian life. If you were to ask most church members about what this meant, you would not get a clear answer. We must be able to defend our faith. John 3:3 (KJV) says, "Jesus answered and said unto him, Verily, verily I say unto thee, Except a man be born, he cannot see the kingdom of God." John 3:5–6 (LB) says,

> Jesus replies What I am telling you so earnestly is this, Unless one is born of water and of the spirit, he cannot enter the kingdom of God. Men can only reproduce human life, but the Holy Spirit gives new life from heaven, so don't be surprised at my statement that you must be born again.

Being born again is how we ask if we are saved. It is very important that we understand that this was the plan of salvation Jesus executed for us at Calvary. We must understand what is required for us to be born again. One thing I think we agree on is that Jesus died on the cross to bring salvation for everyone who will accept him (Luke 14:23 KJV). Acts 19:4–6 reads,

Then said Paul, John verily baptized with the baptism of repentance, saying unto the people, that they should believe on him which should come after him, that is, Jesus Christ. When they heard this, they were baptized in the name of the Lord Jesus. And when Paul had laid his hands upon them, the Holy Ghost came on them; and they spake with tongues and prophesied.

You need to know what Calvary means. How will I accept what was done for me in my own life? Jesus Christ's death, burial, and resurrection are the three steps of Calvary. In 1 Corinthians 15:1–4, we read that these are the three steps to being born again. We must symbolize the same death, burial, and resurrection so we can see Jesus when we are born again. We receive salvation when we respond to John 3:16 (KJV): "For God so loved the world, that he gave his only begotten Son, that whosoever believeth in him should not perish, but have everlasting life." In John 3:3, we read, "Jesus answered and said unto him Verily, verily, I say unto thee, except a man be born again he cannot see the kingdom of God."

This is the best news for all humankind to be back in relationship with their creator since the fall of Adam and Eve. Jesus gave us the answer when he told Nicodemus, "Ye must be born again." Nicodemus was a religious leader and yet could not give a clear concept of what it meant to be born again. The same thing happens to us today. I thank God that the church I attend teaches us to defend our faith by knowing how to give an answer to those who are in error.

This question pops up all the time: how can we be born again? We cannot be born again of a woman. The second birth is a spiritual birth. Jesus said we cannot enter the kingdom of God without being born again; the bottom line is that we cannot be saved. When Peter preached on the day of Pentecost, the message after Calvary all the men present cried out was, "What must we do?" Peter said, "Repent and be baptized every one of you in the name of Jesus Christ for the remission of sins and ye shall receive the gift of the Holy Ghost" (Acts 2:38).

In Acts 2:38, Peter gave them the plan of salvation. Jesus wanted all to be saved and come to repentance. Just like Jesus, Peter was talking to them about being saved. Jesus was our substitute in his death, burial, and resurrection. All we must do is accept what he did by spiritually dying, being buried, and rising again. It is called baptism. There are three baptisms: salvation, water, and baptism into the Spirit.

Salvation is when we repent; we take on his death, a spiritual death. This is when the old man in us dies if we truly repent. We renounce our will forever and vow to live from that moment on according to the will of Jesus Christ. We then have salvation and qualify for heaven. We take on his burial by water baptism in the name of Jesus Christ. Romans 6:4 says, "Therefore we are buried with him by baptism. It must be done by emersion and not by just a sprinkle of water on the top of the head. " Our baptism in the Bible gave us examples such as John the Baptist submerging Jesus in water. This alone should determine our course of action.

The last step is when we partake of the resurrection of Jesus Christ by the infilling of the Holy Spirit. The new life we receive from the Holy Spirit enables us to live as Christians should. So being born again means to first repent of sins, be baptized in the name of Jesus Christ by immersion, and receive the gift of the Holy Spirit. In 1 John 5:8, we read, "And there are three that bear witness in the earth, the spirit, and the water, and the blood and these three agree in one."

The blood covers the sin at repentance, and the water of baptism washes them away thus making us clean for the Spirit to dwell in us. In John 19:34, we read about the Roman soldier thrusting his spear into Jesus and blood and water coming forth. This was to be the cleansing of the nations. It takes blood and water to eradicate sin. Blood is the cleansing agent, and water is the flushing agent.

It takes blood and water to clean the human soul so that it can receive the Spirit of Christ, the Holy Spirit. Peter clarified this in Acts 2:38: "Repent and be baptized for the remission of sins." Paul taught us that we should preach that Jesus Christ died for our sin according to the scriptures and that he was buried and that he rose again the third day.

The gospel of Christ is the death, burial, and resurrection of our Lord Jesus Christ according to the scriptures. We obey the death, burial, and resurrection of Christ by repentance, baptism, and receiving the Holy Spirit. In 2 Thessalonians 1:7–8, we read,

And to you who are troubled rest with us, when the Lord
Jesus shall be revealed from heaven with his mighty angels,
In flaming fire taking vengeance on them that know not
God, and that obey not the Gospel of our Lord Jesus Christ.

Even the Old Testament, a shadow of things to come, teaches us
there were three steps when the priests offered sacrifices on the altar,
which represents salvation. The blood of the animals was caught in
a container for use in the holy place. The flesh of the animal was
consumed with fire. When we repent, we present our bodies as living
sacrifices and our sins are covered by the blood of Jesus. After the
shedding of blood, the priests were ordered to wash at the laver and
to cleanse themselves with water in preparation for entering the holy
place. The laver was a round, fountain- like structure and had a
looking glass in the bottom so the priests could make sure they were
clean after they washed.

Those who are baptized should examine themselves to be sure they
are leaving the world behind forever. The second step of the tabernacle
ministry teaches us about water baptism.

After the cleansing, the priests took fire from the altar and entered
through the veil into the holy place, which was lit only by seven wicks
fed by oil from seven bowls. The wicks had to be lit by the fire brought
by the priest from the brazen altar. The wicks produced light that was
a perfect Holy Spirit, the fire promised to the New Testament believers
in Matthew 3:11. Without the light of the Holy Spirit, we could not
see to live in the holy place, where every Christian should live.

In 1 John 5:8, we read, "There are three that bear witness in the
earth, the spirit, the water, and the blood and these three agree in one."
God sent his Word to heal us and deliver us from self-destruction.
Emanuel means God with us, and he is in us when we are born again.
This is what brings us into a Christmas atmosphere and a new chapter
and story.

The Origins of Christmas

The origins of Christmas are well known and are not particularly
controversial. The question we ask is whether we should be celebrating
it. It is a traditional holiday that originated in paganism and was

incorporated into Christianity in the fourth and fifth centuries. It is not a biblical feast and was never practiced by the first-century church. Do Christmas and Santa upstage Jesus Christ? Jesus never authorized us to have a memorial to celebrate his birth; instead, he instructed us to keep a memorial to his death.

In Luke 22:19 (LB), we read, "Then he took a loaf of bread and when he had given thanked God for it, he broke it apart and gave it to them, saying 'This is my body, given for you, eat it in remembrance of me.'" And 1 Corinthians forbids us from adopting pagan customs in the worship of the true God. Paganism is a doctrine that holds onto behavior motivated by the desire for pleasure and the avoidance of pain; pagans are not Christian, Muslim, Jewish, or nonreligious.

When we get into the economics of Christmas, we find that people are trying to give what they should be giving all year—love for all humankind. The next time the spirit of Christmas hits you, grab hold of it and don't let it go. When you catch yourself giving from the heart, take a picture of yourself and rewind and remind yourself of that moment as you practice it all year long. You will see how we were put here for one another and not just for ourselves. Between credit cards, guilt, stress, and lying to children while focusing on materialistic things, we end up disappointed. December 25 began as the birthday of the sun god, not the Son of God. Mithras was a solar deity of Persian origin identified with the sun.

There were also agrarian cultures that worshipped in important festivals around the end of December. One of the holidays was Saturnalia, which included making and giving small presents. The holiday was observed beginning on December 17, the birthday of Saturn, and ending on December 25, the birthday of Sol Invictus, the Unconquered Sun. These two festivals combined resulted in an extended winter holiday season, not a holy day. Singing "Rudolf the Red-Nosed Reindeer" and "Santa Claus is Coming to Town" only supports the lie being told. "All too well you reject the commandments of God, that you may keep your traditions—making the Word of God of non-effect through your traditions which you have handed down. And many such things you do" (Mark 7:9, 13).

Christ in Christmas

The truth of Christmas will stand tall after all the lies have been told. Let's look at Christmas in today's religious and spiritual point of view. God has given us a different outlook on the holiday. To us, it is a holy day. To us, the Christmas tree is put up to represent the eternal life that Jesus brings. When it is cut down and then put up again, it represents the resurrection of our Lord and Savior. The wreath is a circle that represents God's eternal love. These decorations remind us that Jesus is the reason behind this season.

Gift giving has a deeper meaning. The wise men, the magi, were scholarly foreigners who traveled to see Jesus after his birth; they came bearing gifts of gold, frankincense, and myrrh (verses 1:5, 8:11 AMP). These gifts were connected to the worship of Jesus because of the three symbols of worship in the original temple. Gold has great value and will never be worthless; it is a worthy gift for a king. In the first temple, the vessels and furnishings were covered in gold. The Ark of the Covenant including the mercy seat, where the sacrificial blood was sprinkled, was covered with gold.

Gold has an eternal quality about it being found in heaven and on earth. Our spirits are eternal. It is in us because God put it in us, and it can never be undone. But sin brought a state of death to our spirits. When we bring our gifts of worship to Jesus as our Savior, his gift to us is victory over spiritual death through the gift of eternal life.

There was also frankincense, a milky resin extracted from trees; the ancients used its restorative properties for treating depression. It was used by the high priest on the day of atonement in the holy of holies. The presence of the Lord would appear during the smoke from the frankincense. Revelation 5:8 (LB) reads, "And as he took the scroll the scroll, the twenty- four Elders fell before the Lamb each with a harp and golden vials filled with incense-the prayers of God's people." Psalm 22:3 (LB) reads, "For you are holy. The praises of our fathers surrounded your throne, they trusted you and you delivered them." This scripture tells us how God inhabits the praises of his people. Both these scriptures tell us about healing in our praise, which reverses depression. Jesus gave eternal life to our spirits and peace to our minds

(Isaiah 53:5). Our gift of worship and prayers are lifted to God, and we can receive his gift of blessed peace.

Myrrh is a very fragrant resin produced by a small scraggly tree in North Africa. It was a wound healer because of its strong antiseptic and anti-inflammatory properties. The Chinese have used it medically for centuries. Myrrh was the main ingredient of the anointing oil in the temple. This perfumed oil made anything it touched consecrated and holy to God. In Matthew 26, a woman poured expensive perfume on Jesus's head in preparation for his burial. Myrrh's most famous use was for embalming but also for healing. We recognize Jesus as the gift given by the Father; those who believe can have eternal qualities for their spirits, peace for their souls, and healing for their bodies. This is what we Christians call the gift of eternal proportions giving us God's likeness.

The Story of the Candy Cane

> I wandered if when Jesus planned the candy cane and He knew that you and I would make it. Christmas candy through and through. We buy it everywhere in all sizes and use it everywhere. In Santa's packs and reindeers backs and never gives a care. But Jesus made it special and so many just don't see. The meaning of the candy cane means life for you and me. The shape is of the Shepherds staff and all His, and we are His sheep.
>
> The stripes He bore upon the cross keep us from wrath and grief. The red is for the Saviors blood He shed upon the tree. The white means Jesus life perfect and purity. The candy cane taste sweet. A favorite to us all and makes us want to pass it on to anyone who calls. And so, my friend, this season is drawing very near, So, pass along this candy cane, but let everybody hear, the story of our Savior and His sweet love for us, and how he proved that love by dying upon the cruel cross, the peppermint flavor can represent the hyssop plant that was used for purifying the Bible. So please except this truth I have here in my hand, and you become a part of God's own perfect plan.

Would you like to enter that perfect plan God has for your life? It is a perfect plan for imperfect people. Just pray this prayer and find a church that agrees with your Bible and be baptized in the name of Jesus Christ because Jesus Christ is the name of the Father, Son, and the Holy Spirit. Ask God to fill you with his Spirit. "You have not because you ask not."

Prayer to Receive Jesus Christ as Lord and Savior

Heavenly Father, you said in your Word that if I confess with my mouth and believe in my heart that you raised Jesus Christ from the dead that I would be saved. Father God, I repent of all my sins, and I renounce my past life in the mighty name of Jesus Christ. I come to you and turn from Satan. I believe Jesus Christ died for my sin and for my forgiveness so that I may commune with you, my creator.

Forgive me for not serving you, and make me a new creature. I am yours spirit, soul, and body. Behold, all thing are new.

Now, believe you have received your salvation and thank God for saving you. Thank you, Jesus, for paying my ransom on the cruel cross for my sin!

Revival

It's time to stand up and join the fight This is a war cry calling all warriors to pick up their spiritual weapons and start to fight.

> A revival is the improvement in or strength of something. A turn for the better, upturn, upswing, resurgence. It is an instance of something becoming popular, active or important again. A reestablishment or restoration. It is the resurrection of a person or thing.

This book inspires members of the church body and assists converts. It increases and renews the readers and will have a global effect, a revival. It is evangelizing so people won't die for the lack of God's presence.

Only fools will forever be away from God's presence. They run from him, not to him. Maybe they have never heard of him. Fools are ignorant about who God is. They cause problems especially by inciting others to defy those in authority; they are agents of Satan. They are the walking dead and need reviving. God uses people to punish the disobedient and he "uses them like a whip" (2 Samuel 7:14 Everyday Bible).

To revive them, we need to restore life, consciousness, and strength to their spirits and God's wisdom to their souls. They may have physical strength, but they lack the Spirit that gives boldness and strength to their inner man. We all need to be energized with strength from Jehovah. New converts must be invigorated, revitalized, rejuvenated, and refreshed. Being stimulated spiritually restores our interest in God. When we introduce Jesus Christ to others, we help them reestablish a relationship with him.

We begin to resuscitate the walking dead—thieves, witches, sorcerers, and any other sinners—and rekindle in them a strong desire for and great expectations and hopes for Jehovah. This will help them improve their conditions in life. They will begin to revive themselves through the Word of God and flourish. They start coming back to life and health so God can use them to spread the Word. Jehovah wants them to develop and become successful by investing time in his Word and his will for their lives.

God wants to give you a brand-new conversation—the truth—so you can speak good things into your life and the lives of others and be the best you can be. You can be Christlike and present a new and improved you who will achieve your God-ordained destiny. When you irrigate the ground in your heart with the Word of God by being washed in the Word, you will become a clean vessel ready to be used by God. You will have nutritious words coming out of your mouth. When you delight in the Lord, he will give you the desires of your heart. Don't serve Jehovah God by what you see or hear but develop an up-close and personal relationship with him. Easier said than done, but let's do it. "But be ye a doer of the word and not just a hearer only, deceiving your own selves" (James 1:22 KJV).

Salvation

Salvation is yours, and you must learn how to get others saved. Work out your own salvation with fear and trembling. Ask others, "If you died tonight, would heaven be your home?" God requires us to repent of our sin, confess, and believe. You are now a new creature in Christ Jesus. "Therefore, if any man be in Christ, he is a new creature, old things have passed away: behold all things have become new" (2 Corinthians 5:17).

God has made you a new creature, and your mistakes and sins have gone away. God sees you as a new creature. Your spirit has been made alive unto God. You are like a newborn. You do not have to feel guilty about anything bad you have done because God forgives and forgets that.

When and if you sin or drop the ball again, just admit it, quit it, and get back with it; get back in line with the Word of God. In other words, repent. If you drop the ball, you can recover it by repentance and God's grace giving you what you don't deserve. "And their sins and iniquities will I remember no more" (Hebrews 10:17). God's Holy Spirit is dwelling in you; if you sin, 1 John 1 says, "If we confess our sins, he is faithful and just to forgive us of our sins, and to cleanse us from all unrighteousness through Jesus Christ."

Be sure to accept God's forgiveness and receive what Jesus has already done for you at the cross. Now you are clean through the word (John 5:3). Most important—forgive yourself and don't hold yourself captive to your past.

Let Your Complaints Be Turned into Praise and Thanksgiving

Our praises give God the glory as the four beasts in Revelation 4:8.

> And the four beasts had each of them six wings about him;
> and they were full of eyes within: and they rest not day
> and night, saying Holy, holy, holy Lord God Almighty,
> which was, and is, and is to come.

God likes to be appreciated. He keeps your lying, hardheaded, rebellious, and disobedient self in his grace. Thank God for the blood of Jesus Christ.

Maybe I am just talking about me. I guess I am the only one because everybody else has made it to perfection in Christ. You are going to let me talk about me, aren't you? I'm so glad to be me. Are you glad to be you? Some people want to be someone other than whom God made them to be.

Our kids want to be savage beasts. With all the technology in our society, they want to go back to the age when man's thoughts were continually evil. We still know not what we do. This can bring a lot of sadness into our lives by making bad decisions. Our street corners have turned into memorials for lost loved ones. These memorials are from a lot of sin and some are from disobedience to God or not being taught God's ways. The Lord looks to see whom he can make strong while Satan looks to see whom he may devour. Revelation 4:5 reads, "And out of the throne preceded lightning and thundering and voices: and there were seven lamps of fire burning before the throne, which are the seven Spirits of God." God told Joshua to meditate day and night on the Word so they would be in concert. The four beasts and the twenty elders worshipped God, who created all things for his pleasure (Revelation 4:10–11).

It is a joy to kick it with our creator. When we hang out with God, we are under his protection. Rejoicing in Christ silences the enemy and makes our grief joyful. In 1 John 1:4, we read, "It brings us from a low state of mind and put our minds on things above." Praising God puts our mind on the higher life so we forget about the lower life. Things that pertain to the lower life aim between our legs. Think on things above having the mind of Christ.

Praising God gives me peace when the Holy Spirit leads and guides me. You should build upon God's promises in his Word. God's mercy and faithfulness to us are with Christ, and it is with him that all the promises are. The only way sinners can benefit from God's mercy and faithfulness is by being saved, repenting, and being baptized in water and in spirit. They must first learn God's ways. Sinners don't know that God gives them daily opportunities to come to him. I hear many acknowledging God, but they are reluctant to come to him. They are alive by his grace but dead in their sin.

God's mercy flows through Jesus making the promises of God strong through him. If they confess with their mouths and believe in their hearts that God raised Jesus from the dead, they will be saved. They must be able to withstand correction and submit to authority. It makes our covenant strong with him when we have the covenant of redemption made with him and the covenant of grace made with us in him. David and Solomon were corrected, but they did not lose their inheritances. In 2 Samuel 7:14–15 (KJV), we read,

> I will be his father, and he shall be my son. When he commits iniquity, I will chasten him with the rod of men, and with the stripes of children of men: but my mercy shall not depart away from him, as I took it from Saul, whom I put away before thee.

David's seed endured through generations. Luke 1:27–32 says,

> To a virgin espoused to a man whose name was Joseph, of the house of David; and the virgin's name was Mary. And the angel came in unto her, and said, hail thou that art highly favored, the Lord is with thee: blessed art thou among women. And when she saw him, she was troubled at his saying, and cast in her mind what manner of salutation this should be. And the angel said unto her, Fear not, Mary: for thou hast found favor with God. And, behold thou shalt conceive in thy womb, and bring forth, and shalt call his name Jesus. He shall be great and shall be called the Son of The Highest; and the Lord God shall give unto him the throne of his father David.

Jesus was named the Son of God before he came out of the womb. This story continued in chapter 2, verses 4–11. Every believer is Christ's spiritual seed, which endures forever. Until the end, Christ will have people serving and honoring him while others do not.

We may break his laws by sins of omission and commission; there are as many corruptions as there are people in the church. Sin is a broad area. Every individual has a right to come to the spiritual emergency room, the church, and have a spiritual heart transplant. The issues of life are supposed to flow from our hearts. "I will visit their transgression with a rod." Affliction to God's people is nothing but a rod. It is for our correction, not for our destruction. God has used his rod on me so I would fulfill his purpose in me, and there is nothing I can do about it because he never lies. David was exposed to his neighbors, and all his walls were broken down. When a man can't control his spirit, he is like a defenseless city without walls.

Solomon had the same problem as David did when it came to women. The generational curse came straight to Solomon. Heart problems ran in the family. When posterity degenerates, it falls into disgrace and iniquity and stains glory. We think that God has made man in vain because we see so many die young. I have seen people who had short lives but accomplished more than did those who lived longer. Some never make it to their first birthday. A lot of people prefer not to get old. They had more communions with God and glorified God and are ready to die. Some die young for not honoring parents and by having no sense of direction. People in the armed forces understand death and are readier than most are to die. The church's armed forces are more equipped because God fight their battles. God's people have angels of the Lord encamped around them to deliver them from evil. No evil shall befall them, nor will plague or calamity come near their dwelling in Jesus's name.

Many do not know why they were born having no communion with God. We should all ask ourselves, *Why was I born?* We all have purposes, but we have to discover them through Christ Jesus as we study the Bible. Some people believe that human life evolved; they fail to produce evidence for why we are here. They don't tell us where our intelligence comes from. Our creativity comes from being Christlike. When man creates, we are in God's image. God created the earth by speaking. They can't explain evil. Some speak on Hellenism trying to explain man's condition. The Word of God explains the evil of the world and where it originated. People who don't worship God are ignorant about who he is and do not serve him.

To understand something, you must be of it and into it. You can't judge from the outside looking in. We see people getting blessed, but we must remember that God will do for you what he did for them. God is not a respecter of persons. Stop coveting what someone else has and develop a personal relationship with him. Obey him even in tough times. You develop faith and courage by reading and meditating on his Word with a sincere heart while having a personal relationship with him.

God is spirit, and man is physical. People get hurt and spread that hurt around, but they don't want to develop and go through the process of becoming children of God. We call it conversion. God gave Adam and Eve the Tree of Life, which signified eternal life, and the Tree of the Knowledge of Good and Evil. Adam and Eve had not yet received immortal life in the garden; it was meant for them upon their obedience. Jesus came on the scene to clean up the mess man made and brought us eternal life.

God will never forsake you. God has covenant with those he has chosen. The more I fellowship with God, the closer we become. God told Adam and Eve that if they ate from the Tree of the Knowledge of Good and Evil, they would die, but they ate from it anyway and lost their lives of peace, joy, and happiness; sin and suffering came to humans. Disobedience brings suffering. Much witchcraft and sorcery are going on, and many children are dying because grown-ups disobey God causing generational curses. People seem not to understand the curses witchcraft and sorcery bring. God had given man a perfect character from the beginning. God is perfecting that as we grow in Christ. Man is learning to choose what is right. Our nation is becoming like an orphan learning from his or her mistakes. We learn that God's ways are the best ways.

"Our character has knowledge, wisdom, purpose, ability that are properly controlled and developed through our choices" (World Tomorrow Why Were You Born). God recreated himself in us, who have spirits, bodies, and souls. God's spirit in us animates us. When we study God's Word and receive revelations, we began to grow spiritually and become more like him. When we are born again, we are born into God's family, and we must deny self so we will not self-destruct. When we walk with God, he reveals to us how we are being deceived and how the enemy is trying to take us out. We will begin to understand the purpose and the meaning of our lives when we see how the enemy is trying to stop our development. God is trying to deliver us from the pitfalls, temptations, and delusions the enemy dangles in our faces. God brings us from darkness into his light to keep us from stumbling and falling into the enemy's traps. The more people blaspheme, scoff, and scorn God, the more we should bless him and give him glory, honor, and praise.

Raise a Child

I am fortunate to present my book to warn the world at such a time as this. Mental kidnapping is all over the world, but it started in the home. I was raised in a Christian home by JB and Teretha Treadwell. When I was growing up, I was an obedient child for the most part. Everybody who came to our house told my parents that they had done a nice job with their kids. The fear placed in us at home showed as obedience. It was a fear of God and our parents, who had the strap.

My mom had a formula for all children having had eight. She would talk us or whip us into submission. Kids know when they are being hardheaded and rebellious. When other kids would come around acting out of place, my mother would want to meet with their parents or take them home to see why they were acting as they did. She didn't allow any disobedience from other kids or from hers. She would tell the parents that they better get them before she did. My mom saw what other parents did not see in their kids and told them in front of their kids.

Other parents knew it was all right for their kids to be at Mrs. Teretha's house because she was not having it. I believe she was sharing God's Word and using the kids to witness to their parents. My mom stayed in the presence of God, and two days out of the week and all day Sunday, she kept us in God's presence. We kids sang in the choir, but I never thought I was ushering people into God's presence. I tell my brothers and sisters that we did not know what we were doing at church but that our mom knew. She took us to church so we could receive the promises of God.

All eight of us kids were saved at young ages and were kept under God's wings and in the palm of his hand so we could attain hope in Christ Jesus. As we grew older, we were given chores. Mom nourished and disciplined us until each one of us was old enough to be guided by the older ones. My father worked at Amour Meats in stores across Memphis to provide for his family, and sometimes, he butchered cows, deer, or hogs on the side for extra money and meat in Arkansas and Mississippi. When Mom finished weaning a child, she would do homecare and cleaning and sometime nanny the boss's daughter. When Mom had to go to work, she assigned our oldest sister, Nora, to oversee us and the house. She was punished if things were not in order when Mom came home. Oh boy, I did not want to be Nora if the house was not clean or something happened. This program worked out fine when we were young, but as some of us reached our teen years, we thought we were all grown up. We learned that if we thought we were grown, we had to get our own.

At times, Mom came home to find thing not done that we should have taken care of. She would ask why this or that was not done, and she would take a nap so she would be refreshed when she got up, declared war, and started whipping our behinds. She would herd all of us into a corner, and for some strange reason, I would always end up in front pushed by my brothers and sisters, who were trying to evade the strap. If we got out of line, she had torture treatments for us. She would throw us in the attack or put our supposedly grown behinds out in the cold.

Daddy would come home and find his children in the attic or on the porch in the cold because of our disobedience. Mom didn't put up with mutiny in our house. He would ask why we were in the cold, and we would say Mom told us to go there. He would talk to her for a moment and say, "All y'all come on in here." When I got older, I believed that they were playing the good guy bad guy routine on us. Daddy opposed it, but he could not go against the grain. The Bible says honor your mother and father, and our going to church helped keep us safe from a hostile takeover. Dad would tell us to do what Mom told us to do.

God's spiritual seed was planted in us all at an early age along with chastisement from a mother and father. God was with us as children, and we really did not realize how great a seed had grown in us. Jehovah God protected us and gave us all special talents and abilities. We were all baptized before age twelve. God gave all eight of us a light to shine in us, on us, around us, and for us, and that light is still shining in all of us until this day and in our children and grandchildren. My daughter Kimberly really took to teaching in school and at church. "Correction and punishment make children wise, but those left alone will disgrace their mother" (Proverbs 29:15 Everyday Bible).

Moving Forward in Faith with Patience

Faith keeps us in concert with God. God's promises never fail because he never fails. When we pray and believe, we receive what we desire. Jesus said in Matthew 9:29, "According to your faith be it unto you." These spiritual laws work for us when we put the Word of God in our hearts. When we believe the Word, speak it, and act on it, we receive what God promised.

We should never let the enemy slip doubt and unbelief into our thoughts while we are waiting on our answers to manifest. We must be patient for what we pray for, watch what we say and believe, and not talk ourselves out of it because we walk by faith, not by sight. When we second- guess God's Word, we end up like waves tossed around by the wind. We go in circles from belief to unbelief. James 1:6–7 reads, "We stumble in our faith, and as a result we can't receive from God." This is when we call on our superhero patience, one fruit of the Spirit. Patience helps us as we are waiting for our desires. We use faith to get the victory over the world, but we use our superhero patience to remain strong in God's Word and his promises when we are under pressure. We must have faith and patience to get the job done. If we persist, we will succeed.

Hebrews 12:12 states, "Let us run with patience the race that is set before us, looking unto Jesus the author and the finisher of our faith." When we are patient, we endure pain in difficult times and go through annoyance calmly. Our patience will help us achieve more than we could without that gift. "Be not slothful, but followers of them who through faith and patience inherit the promises" (Hebrews 6:12). We must calmly await an outcome. Adding faith and patience sums up to victory.

"The trying of our faith worketh patience. But let patience have her perfect work, that ye may be perfect and entire, wanting nothing." Patience and faith help us handle our difficult times. Whatever we are believing God for, we must believe we receive it and act as though it is already ours. We should not worry, fret, or be anxious about anything; we should not have a care after we have prayed and cast all our cares on God. When we make our confessions to God, he reacts to his Word. God chose us, and he knows we have the heart for the job and what we need to do it. We must have the thoughts and feelings of Christ.

Stay in faith and get the victory. If you fall into doubt and unbelief, just repent it; admit it, quit it, and get back with it; get back in line with the Word of God. Get back in the race and hold fast to your confessions of faith. Decide to walk by faith and practice faith. Your faith comes by hearing the Word of God. The enemy will always try to get you to fall into doubt and unbelief, so you need to quench his fiery darts and keep moving forward in faith. When the enemy comes, just stick to the faith fight and stay on course. The battle is not yours; it's the Lord's. Don't let the enemy kidnap you mentally and take your victory. Satan is a con man who won't give up trying to get you to see it his way. We must keep resisting the devil and stand in faith and patience.

The more we let patience have its way, the stronger we will become. Then we will become perfectly and fully developed and lack nothing. James 1:4 (AMP) tells us, "So, stay strong in the Lord and in the power of His might." Keep saying words of power, love, and life to produce good things into your and others' lives, and wait patiently on the victory or the manifestation. Take your stand and become one of those who through faith and patience inherits the promises by praying, confessing, believing, and receiving God's favor.

Favor

We need to be instructed in true blessings. We seek to be happy, and our happiness will consist of the favor of God, not the wealth of this world. The Word says that blessed is the man whose iniquity is forgiven. We should focus more on getting our sin forgiven than on gaining wealth. This is the fundamental privilege from which all other blessings flow. He was pardoned of his transgressions, so the punishment that comes with sin is canceled. I always feel relieved when I confess my sin.

Sin carries the weight of guilt, shame, and condemnation. If we have a heavy burden, it is the covering of sin. Hiding sin can be burdensome because we are afraid of being caught naked, so we are ashamed. We use all kinds of fig leaves to try to cover our sins just like Adam and Eve ducking and hiding in the garden of Eden. God already knows, and maybe we will pass the test next time if not unto death.

Revelation 3:18 says, "I counsel thee to buy of me gold tried in the fire, that thou mayest be rich; and white raiment, that thou mayest be clothed, and that the shame of thy nakedness does not appear; and anoint thine eyes-salve, that thou mayest see." David and Solomon had the favor of God. Solomon built the temple, but God was with him. The scripture says, "Except the Lord build the house they labor in vain that build it." God chose David to be king even though he had a poor education. David was a descendant of the prince of the tribe of Judah. He was a shepherd, not a soldier. This lets us know that if God is for us, no one can be against us. David and Moses were taken from the sheepfold. God honors those who are humble and will bring them to the forefront.

God gives you a thoughtful inspection. David and Solomon showed compassion to their flocks especially those who needed care the most and kept them from going astray. David was skillful and faithful. He fed, ruled, taught, guided, and protected his flock like a good pastor. He loved his neighbor as himself. Even the people felt the heart of David. "From the heart reaches the heart." David was the image of Christ, the good shepherd. Even when David sinned, God pardoned him and covered him with the robe of righteousness just as Jesus died for my sin and covered me with his precious blood.

He was forgiven as far as the east is from the west; that is how far he has removed our transgressions from us. God says that if we confess our sin, he will forgive us and cleanse us through Jesus Christ. We were made righteous in Christ Jesus, who took up our iniquity. Who never sins? When we are saved, we do not lie.

We should not pretend to be loving when we have hate in our hearts. Those who hide their convictions by keeping silent cannot see the evil of their sin; they try to think of things that will not burden their consciences. They are not truly sorry about their sin and keep sinning. These people torment themselves rather than taking the easy way—believing that Jesus Christ died for us. God gave us a way out of our guilt, shame, and condemnation and gave us rest for our souls by repentance. David said in Psalm 32:5, "I acknowledge my sin unto thee, and mine iniquity have I not hid. I said I will confess my transgressions, unto the Lord; and thou forgive the iniquity of my sin Selah."

To find peace of mind, we should confess our sins so God can forgive them. Jesus Christ freed me from guilt, shame, and condemnation and declared me blameless. When we repent of our sin, God faithfully forgives and cleanses us through Jesus Christ. God forgives us as the father of the Prodigal Son forgave his son after a life of riotous living. God's love for us is so strong that he will forgive even murder. We should repent with a sincere heart. Sometimes, we go out into the world and come back looking like something the cat dragged in. God sees us from afar and runs to meet us with his love.

Christians should be praying people all the time, not just when trouble comes their way. When we have prayers laid up in heaven, the floods of life will not overtake us. Psalm 91:7 tells us, "It will not come nigh thee." God will keep us from danger, evil, and trouble and make everything come out in our favor. We must pray and give thanks to the Lord in advance and on credit. God wishes all to be saved and come to repentance; he wants us to "strengthen our brethren" (Luke 22:32).

We need counsel from our spiritual guides so that we do not miss our many blessings. Satan wants us to be alone so he can attack us and keep us bound in sin. When we are alone, we don't have anyone to hold us accountable for our actions. Thank God for the ministers and the brothers and sisters of God.

This is another way that God leads and guides us into all truths and to where our treasures are. We stay at Jesus's feet because faith comes by hearing the Word of God. Some goats will try to buck the system God laid out for them; that is why we need so much prayer. The goat mentality will end only in sorrow. Goats fight the answer. When we stay plugged in to God, his mercy and grace will pursue us. We ought to let grace and mercy catch up with us and just walk in them. I'm going to let them catch up with me because I need them. At least I know they have my back.

We must have holy joy when we praise God because it is the heart and soul of the praise we give God. The joy of the Lord is our strength. Thankful praise is holy joy. I don't understand how a person can be so full of God's goodness and not give him the praise due him. It is not as if we really deserve it because we could have been dead and gone sleeping in our graves.

Some praise God to see what they can get out of him. They seek his hand but not his face. Few live to his glory. God doesn't want spiritual wimps. We must trust him and stand for him in hard times. God said, "But the cowardly, unbelieving, abominable, murders, sexual immoral, sorcerers, idolaters, and all liars shall have their part in the lake which burns with fire and brimstone, which is the second death" (Revelation 21:8). God wants true worshippers who have the Shadrach, Meshach, and Abednego kind of faith. We must develop the kind of living faith we will need in these last days. Our God is the Father of the faithful. Psalm 34:19 states, "Many are the afflictions of the righteous but the Lord delivereth him out of them all." God saves us from the enemy's traps and snares. We should meditate on being faithful like Abraham. God told him, "For I know that you fear God, since you have not withheld your son, your only son from me" (Genesis 22:12). Let's be faithful to God as he is faithful to us.

God created the heavens and the earth. God said it, and it was so. Jesus came to show us how to operate in the Word being the Word made flesh. He came to bring us back to God and show us how to make our confession to him. We have to say what God says and agree with him. We must establish God's Word here on earth. If the condition of our hearts is right, the law of confession will always work. When our hearts are lined up with God's Word, that can change our lives.

C HAPTER 4

Social Wellness

Take Heed of My Ways

We must be careful of the wicked with sin in their roots and branches. They have no fear of God, and they break his laws. The wicked think they are right; they will not acknowledge their evil deeds. They call evil good and good evil. They do not see the dangers in their evil practices. They don't know that evil will destroy them. They engage in licentious sexual activities.

God gave us all liberty, but some think they are doing justice. In time, their iniquity will convict them. Their cursed branches spring from a root of bitterness and make them defy God. Their words are full of lies. They plot day and night and make their schemes look and sound good. Some groups are formed just to create evil. Their hearts are hard, and they have no fear of God or convictions. They do evil, not good. The applaud other evil people.

Saints do not think bad thoughts about God's kingdom. They should never think God approves of sin. Some people think God puts up with sin because he has put up with their mess for so long. God's sun and rain fall on the just and the unjust. God is a faithful and just God. He does not change as men do. God's wisdom is unsearchable. His judgment is deeper than our understanding. God protects us and provides the things we need so we can abound in every good work and charitable donation.

This is the favor of God, and our role is to put all our trust in God and to be kept in the palm of his hand. When God supplies our wants, they become our benefits; Psalm 103 says, "Forget not all His benefits." God wants to enlarge and enlighten our souls so that our desires will be gratified and our capacities will be filled. God will give us all we need to enlighten and enlarge our souls. God has furnished us with all spiritual blessings. We should have gracious souls and always be in position to receive and desire more.

Philippians 4:18 says, "I have all and abound." Joys will flow like a river. Thank God that I have all and abound with divine joy and pleasure. Thank you, Lord, for rivers of pleasures. Pleasures of faith are pure rivers and pleasant like clear water and sparkle like crystal. The Holy Spirit gives us rivers of living water and wisdom, knowledge, and unspeakable joy.

When we walk in the light, God gives us grace and shows us how he appreciates us. God sees us in his glory. God gives us everything that satisfies our understanding. Jesus Christ said, "Sanctify them through thy truth thy word is truth." We communicate with God with his Word, and we receive his grace because we show our love to him. Saints should pray for one another and not have exaggerated opinions of themselves that bring impurities into the kingdom of God. We lift our souls to God in prayer by praying his promises back to him. God's promises should be the foundation of our prayers. We remind God of his Word, and we should always clear the way to the throne room of God by repenting of our sin.

Two things confirm all the promises. The first is the perfection of God's nature; we value the character of he who promised it: "God is not a man that He should lie neither the son of man that He should repent hath He said, and shall He not do it and hath He spoken, and shall He not make it good." The second is the agreeableness of all he says and does with the perfection of his nature. All the paths of the Lord are life and peace, and his promises are mercy and truth because they are like himself—good and upright. God's promises are his will for us; they will direct us in our service to him. God causes our thoughts to become agreeable to his will so that our plans succeed.

Ask God to point out the right way to go. Fix your thoughts on the promises that fit your situation. If you are not born again, you will be taught how to reconcile with God, become grounded in his peace, have a clear conscience, and gain eternal life. "Today I have set before your life and death a blessing and a curse." God gave us a multiple-choice question and its answer. He said, "Choose life that both thou and thy seed may live." Pleasing the Lord by choosing life will give you peace of mind. God will begin to show you secret things when you covenant with him. God wants sincere lovers because sincerity will be your best security in the worst times. We pray that God will strengthen us against the troubles and temptations that destroy our peace. Every time we are tempted to sin, we ought to remind ourselves of the vows we made to God when we were saved. When you said, "Lord God, if you just help me out of this situation,

I promise I will _____," you know what you promised.

The Power of Our Words

Remember how we told God that we would stop saying words of doubt and unbelief? We need to make a list of things we will never say again. We need to stop holding ourselves captive by negative words. This starts with our thoughts. Everything we do begins with a thought. When we have evil thoughts in our minds, we should cover our mouths. Our words are powerful; once we speak them, we will have what we say whether good or bad, whether blessings or curses in our and others' lives. God wants us to speak his Word and be a blessing. Proverbs 25:11 says, "A word fitly spoken is like apples of gold in pictures of silver." Our words should uplift one another, not tear each other down. We should stop speaking curse words toward God's anointed that will bounce off them and boomerang right back at us. Romans 10:10 tells us, "For with the heart man believes unto righteousness and with the mouth confession is made unto salvation." We confessed with our mouths and believed in our hearts that God raised Jesus Christ from the dead. We are to be fountains of living water and stop letting negative words and words of doubt come out of our mouths. We must stop this death talk and speak life more abundantly. John 7:38 says, "He that believeth on me as the scriptures has said, out of his belly shall flow rivers of living water." Sometimes, our mouths can be so filthy that we need some mountain-moving faith to be delivered from our mouths. We must manage our thoughts and emotions better and think twice and speak once. There is nothing so provoking to God than disobedience, when we set our wills in competition with his. I needed some of that mountain- moving teaching that started with Mark 11:23 (KJV).

> For verily I say unto you, That whosoever shall say unto this mountain, Be thou removed, and be thou cast into the sea; and shall not doubt in his heart, but shall believe that those things which he saith shall come to pass; he shall have whatsoever he saith.

We should listen to what comes out our mouths and ask ourselves if we really mean it. We will have what we say. In the garden, Adam named all the animals; everything he called them they were. We must be careful especially when talking to our children and our spouses. Our words have power; things will become whatever we call them.

When wrong words come out of our mouths, we should say, "I renounce, reject, and repent of every word that has ever preceded out my mouth against you, God, and your operation. I cancel its power, and I dedicate my mouth to speak excellent and right things. My mouth shall utter truth for I am the righteousness of God in Christ Jesus, I am complete in Him" (*Prayers That Avail Much for Men*, Prayer; To Watch what I say). Be like David when he told God to "Set a watch O Lord before my mouth keeps the doors of my lips that I might not sin against thee."

Rebellion and stubbornness are as bad as sin, witchcraft, and idolatry. When we disobey God, we become unfit and unruly.

> O generation of vipers, how can ye being evil, speak good things? For out of the abundance of the heart the mouth speaks. A good man out of the good treasure of his heart bringeth forth good things: an evil man out the evil treasure of his heart brings forth evil things. But I say unto you. That every idle word that men shall speak, they shall give account thereof in the Day of Judgment. For by thy words thou shalt be justified, and by thy words thou shall be condemned. (Matthew 12:34–37)

Whatever is in your heart in abundance will come out of your mouth and will set your life in that direction because it is your confession. "He that has no rule over his own spirit is like a city that is broken down and without walls" (Proverbs 25:28). God gave us his Word to instruct, convict, correct, and train us. Every scripture is profitable for instruction, reproof, and conviction of sin. "For correction of error and discipline in obedience and for training in righteousness in holy living, in conformity to God's will in thought, purpose, and action" (2 Timothy 3:16 AMP).

Our words have the power to take us where we are trying to go and change our hearts. Romans 10:10 states, "For with the heart man believeth unto righteousness; and with the mouth confession is made unto salvation." When we pray for healing, we have to confess and believe we will receive it. Grace gives us the opportunity to receive what we desire. We confess and release the faith in our hearts by speaking. We must turn our believing into speaking God's Word. Our words have us in the condition we are in. If we confess with our mouths and believe in our hearts that we can't, then we can't; that is a spiritual law. "Where is boasting then? It is excluded. By what law? Of works? Nay: but by the law of faith" (Romans 3:27). Romans 8:2 tells us, "For the law of the Spirit of life in Christ Jesus hath made me free from the law of sin and death." Our words build or destroy us. What others say about us is not important; what we say about ourselves is important.

Don't leave others' negative words spoken over you hanging in the atmosphere. Just say that they are not yours and confess and believe what God says about you. "But I say unto you, that every idle word that men shall speak, they shall give account thereof in the day of judgment. For by thy words thou shalt be justified, and by thy words thou shalt be condemned" (Matthew 12:36–37).

No one can keep us from our God-ordained destinies but us. We must read and believe scripture and then act as though whatever we are confessing is coming to pass. The only things that keep us from our destinies are our mouths and our disobedience. We must feed faith with the Word of God and do the work of God. God wants us to attend to his Word as nurses attend to their patients. He wants us to pay close attention to it. Proverbs 4:21–22 says, "Let them not depart from thine eyes; keep them in the midst of thine heart. For they are life unto those that find them and health to all their flesh."

Put your confidence in God's Word. Believe in the power of God's Word that comes out of your mouth. God is alive and working in you. God's powerful Word formed the heavens and the earth and gave life. Say, "Let the weak say I am strong" (Joel 3:10). You must call those things that be not as though they were. In the middle of sin, say, "Lord God, thank you for delivering me from …" whatever you are trying to get delivered from. Always say what God says about you.

The truth of God's Word changes the facts. It might be a fact that you have cancer, but it is not truth. John 17:17 says, "Sanctify them through thy truth, thy word is truth." Deuteronomy 30:19 tells us, "I have set before your life and death, blessing and cursing therefore choose life." When we choose God's Word, we choose life. We marinade in God's Word in our spirit man believing it and speaking it and standing on it. Then we must rest in his Word. Jesus said, "My words are spirit and they are life" (John 6:63). Stop talking death and speak words of love and life into your and others' lives. When you choose God's Word, you choose God's will.

Meditate on These Scriptures

> A man shall eat good by the fruit of his mouth He that kept his mouth keepeth his life: but he that openeth wide his lips shall have destruction. (Proverbs 13:2–3)
>
> A man's belly shall be satisfied with the fruit of his mouth; and with the increase of his lips shall he be filled. Death and life are in the power of the tongue: and they that love it shall eat the fruit thereof. (Proverbs 18:20–21)
>
> A wholesome tongue is a tree of life: but perverseness therein is a breach in the spirit. (Proverbs 15:4)
>
> A good man out of the good treasure of his heart bringeth forth that which is good; and an evil man out of the evil treasure of his heart bringeth forth that which is evil: for of the abundance of the heart the mouth speaks. (Luke 6:45)
>
> But I say unto you, that every idle word that men shall speak, they shall give account thereof in the Day of Judgment. For by thy words thou shalt be justified, and by thy words thou shalt be condemned. (Matthew 1:36–7)

God Spanks His Children

Father God chastens us for our own good. Many children are disobedient, and that disobedience can have deep roots; that can make it very difficult for them to reconcile themselves to God's will. Disobedient children will face a lot of heartache and pain in the future. God wants us to see and hear what is wrong with us when we are corrected and come under his discipline. We are his children. When I was in the world, I did not know that all God was trying to do was bless me. God wants to magnify and mature us when he corrects and tries us. We don't deserve God's grace; that fact should not be overlooked.

Warning comes before destruction, and a haughty spirit before a fall. We must take notice of these chances from the voice of God as messages from heaven. Happy is the man whom God corrects and thus improves. Correction is evidence of our being children of God, who sets us apart from the world. God's correction will draw us closer to him and to the Bible for his glory. God's spankings should comfort us. We should stop rebuking what God is trying to do in our lives and start binding and rebuking the devil. All God wants to do is bless us and keep us safe.

We instinctively know the truth about God, but we fight it. Salvation comes to those who know and do God's will. It is a sin to know what is right but not do it. We must be doers of the Word. We can choose to practice truth and righteousness or sin and death. Doctors ask each other, "How is your practice?" We should ask each other, "How is your practice Christlike?" I choose to be a slave to righteousness rather than falsehood. God wants us to obey him, and he gives us his mercy and peace.

Jesus Christ was the mighty son of God with the holy nature of God himself. God wants us to be encouraged, uplifted, and motivated so we can be blessings to one another. I want to help God invite all who believe to heaven. If we stick with it, we will find life through trusting God. God is separate from sin; sinners see God daily but walk away from him. God put knowledge in their hearts, and they know it, so there will be no excuses when they stand before God on Judgment Day. So we should not worry about anything. It is promised that as affliction and trouble set in or reoccur, deliverance shall be graciously repeated by God as often as he pleases. "In six troubles he shall be ready to deliver thee, yea and in seven, there shall no evil touch thee." Job 5:9 tells us, "Which doeth great things, and unsearchable, and marvelous things without number." Whatever trouble you may encounter will not hurt you because God has your back.

God's Protection

We should not be afraid when we are taken under God's special protection. Whatever things people say or do to you will not affect you. When Goliath told David what he would do to him, David encouraged himself that God was in him. We can't keep ourselves free of calamity, reproach, and false accusations, but God can hide us under his wings and in the palm of his hand. He will set us on a cleft where we cannot be reached. David could not fit into the battle armor because it did not fit him, but God has given us one-size-fits-all armor. David let the peace of God rule his heart when he faced Goliath. He had the perfect love that casts out fear. God's peace surpasses all understanding and gives us serenity, security, and hope in God.

I believe that daily prayer, praise, and devotional time with God saved me when I fell nine stories while roofing. It also saved me from an awful death and traumatic injuries. Spending time with God every morning praying over myself and my family helps protect me from hurt, harm, and danger. Pray for ministries at your church, pastors, teachers, evangelists and the lost. Pray for the United States, our president, and the world. I pray the Hedge of Protection prayer and numerous others over all these as we call many by name before the Father. Say this prayer and get personal by putting your name in the blanks.

Hedge of Protection Prayer

> Father, in the name of Jesus, we lift _____ to you and pray a hedge of protection around him/her. We thank you Father, that You are a wall of fire roundabout _____ and that you set Your angels round about him/her.
>
> We thank You, Father, that _____ dwells in the secret place of the Highest and abides under the shadow of the Almighty. We say to You, you are his/her refuge and

fortress, in you will he/she trust. You cover _____ with your feathers and under your wings shall he/she trust. _____ shall not be afraid of the terror by night or the fiery dart that flies by day. Only with his/her eyes will _____ behold and see the reward of the wicked.

Because _____ has made You, Lord his/her refuge and fortress, no evil shall befall him/her—no accident will overtake him/her. Neither shall any plague or calamity come near him/her. For you give your angels charge over _____ to keep him/her in all your ways.

Father, because you have set your love upon _____; therefore, will You deliver him/her. _____ shall call upon You, and You will answer him/her. You will be with him/her in troubles and will satisfywith long life and show him/her Your salvation. Not a hair of his/her head shall perish. (Zachariah 2:5; Psalm 91:8–12, 34:7, 91:14–16, 91:1–2; Luke 21:18; Psalm 91:4–5, from *Prayers that Avail Much*, Word Ministries, Harrison House, Tulsa, Oklahoma)

This is how we should look at any situation because the Holy Spirit is in us and God will never forsake us. When we escaped our Egypt, our bondage, everlasting God kept us in his hand. He is not a sometimes God.

Our day is like a thousand years to him. As soon as we were born, we began to die. The longer we live, the closer we come to death's door.

When we are born again, we repent of our sin and gain the confidence we need to win. We need to abort sin and that coward mentality and stop running from God and run to him. This lets us recognize our sins and faults. We should repent quickly so we don't get caught up in guilt, shame, and condemnation. We must keep God on the scene and let his will be done here on earth as it is in heaven.

We know we will die, so we should be prepared for that. Only God knows the number of our days. We must not act as though God is not paying attention to us as we try to hide sins that go no further than the heart. These sins show up and convict our spirits when they are discovered. The enemy makes the beginning of sin look enticing, but he never shows us the end. Sin brings spiritual death, and sometimes it could end in physical death. We must look at ourselves as though we are going to live forever spiritually. The Israelites spent thirty-eight years in the wilderness sinning while they murmured and complained. They had high hopes of a joyful life in Canaan, but it turned into sadness and depression. They were trapped in the wilderness and could not escape. We become trapped when we don't trust in God.

God brought the Israelites out of Egypt and gave them everything they needed, but they still complained. The world is a wilderness we go through year after year instead of moving forward into the things of God. I learned a lot by reading about the Israelites, and I have learned to follow God. They had a visible cloud to lead them. All they had to do was to stand still and see the salvation of the Lord.

Can you imagine wasting forty years of your life murmuring and complaining instead of trusting in God? God will finish what he started in our lives. Moses could not enter the Promised Land because of his disobedience. Most of the Israelites died in their seventies or eighties. We must ask God to teach us to number our days. When we receive the grace God gives us, and we should appreciate it every day. We know how life can be snatched away suddenly. Moses and Aaron trusted God, but they were cut off from crossing into the Promised Land. We are on assignment, and when our assignment is up, we should thank God for the ride; we should do it heartily and not shuck and jive. We must ask God to show us the path to walk and to give us his peace to carry us through life's ups and downs. We must ask God for mercy and to let his will be done here on earth in our lives as it is in heaven. Lord, let your grace make my face shine with your joy so I can give you glory by working out my salvation. Then I can rest in you and enjoy my victory.

When we live a life plugged in to God, our source, we will be safe under his protection as he sustains us and always gives us peace of mind. We do this by dwelling in the secret place of the highest. We shouldn't let anything contrary to God invade our secret place. The more we study and meditate on God's Word, the more we will be in him and he in us. Studying God's Word feeds his Spirit in us. "Draw nigh to God and He will draw nigh to you." Put your whole heart into service to God, who will protect you. Our lives in Christ are protected by divine grace that keeps us away from Satan's traps.

When we are under God's wings, we will hear his voice and learn about him. We will feel comfortable under his protection. He protects us as a bulletproof vest protects its wearer. We will not fear or be tormented when we are in danger. We will not be afraid for the terror by night, nor for the arrow that flies by day (Psalm 91:5). Staying in God's presence will keep us in perfect peace.

Just think that you are a king surrounded by the FBI, the secret service, and all of God's angels armed and ready to protect you from evil. Man can harm the body but not the spirit of life. Thousands die all around us, but death won't touch us. God has a purpose and plan for us while we live. Hebrews 2:15 (KJV) tells us "not to be subject to bondage as many do all their lifetime through fear of death. And deliver them who through fear of death were all their life time subject to bondage." The valleys of the shadows of death cannot harm you; remember that they are only shadows. "The love of God has been shed abroad in your heart by the Holy Spirit and His love abides in you richly, we must keep ourselves in the kingdom of light, in love, and in the word, and the wicked one touches us not" (Romans 5:5; 1 John 4:16, 5:18, from *My Personal Confessions*).

We Might Be Cast Down but Not Out

Sometimes, we are cast down by others with gossiping, backbiting, and the cares of this world, but we should not care; God will not forsake us. He loves his creation so much that he set up blockades on the road of life to keep us from hurt, danger, and hell. We are all valuable in God's eyes because we are a part of him. To God, a soul is worth all the riches on earth. God sent his Son to die on the cross for our sin debt. God redeems all who receive him.

God is growing in all his ministers and prophets and showing them how to deal with all our Supreme Court judgments and convictions for those who receive those laws in their hearts. God's enemies want to flood the church with these laws, but the church has only God's laws. We must stand firm on his Word and the power of the Holy Spirit. When they come, they will have to take off their shoes, their abominations, because they will be standing on holy ground. God loves the sinner but despises the sin. Some men possessed by demons enjoy destroying the church and worshippers. We as saints should keep our focus on God and the work set before us. If God could destroy Pharaoh and the Egyptians, he can certainly take care of our foes. He can grant us victory over them. He uses those in authority to do his will.

God promised in the garden that the seed of the woman would break the serpent's head. I see women getting ready for the battle. Women have a deep hatred of liars, and they are tired of deceit. They are running from one lie to another (lesbianism). They leave unfaithful husbands but then marry women. I don't know what is up with the men who are descendants of the tribe of Benjamin, who were sons of Belial, a fallen angel, a personification of wickedness and ungodliness (Judges 19:11). Read in Judges 21 how some escaped, and it will show you where the down low came from. The Israelites defeated the tribe of Benjamin, some of whose members ran into the hills and escaped; they were possibly the sons of Belial. The Israelites would not give them their wives. In Judges 21:18–25, Israel gave the Benjamites wives so they would not be without a tribe. The wives of Shiloh married sons of Belial, who were wicked. This could be the reason women love wicked men. In those days, there was no king; all did as they chose.

God gave us his Word and promised to give us faith and the hope we need for victory over our difficulties. God gave us many examples in the Bible of his power and strength. He altered nature by drying up streams and overflowing the banks of the Jordan River. He made water come out of rocks. Baptism by immersion signifies the death, burial, and resurrection of Jesus Christ. God will draw us to his light. He has a life already prepared for us if we will walk with him. He knows how to get us where we need to be. He will save you from your enemies because he is faithful, and we should want to be faithful to him.

God's covenant with Abraham is still going on today. God was keeping his covenant with Noah and his sons when he said, "I will establish my covenant with you; neither shall all flesh be cut off any more by waters of a flood, neither shall there anymore be a flood to destroy the earth" (Genesis 9:11). God wants to be on our side like Nationwide Insurance. He will keep his covenant with us. Every time we see a storm, we should remember the rainbow of that covenant; it confirm his promise to us.

God is not mad at you; he is mad about you. Just the thought of the pretty colors of the rainbow should give you hope of the victory you are seeking. Remember Joseph with his coat of many colors and what he went through and how he came out. He knows that the imagination of man's heart is evil from his youth; "Neither will I again smite anymore everything living as I have done." All God's people need to stop worrying about what they are going to do and put their faith and confidence in him. We should be asking God, "What are you going to do about it?" and get out of his way. Do as I do and ask God to "Plead my cause O Lord" (Psalm 35:1). We should read and pray Psalm 35 and let God take care of our adversary.

The Fool

Fools and atheists are further from God than anyone else, but they are not cast out of God's goodness. They curse and blaspheme God because of their ignorance. They are very open about showing how uninformed they are about God. People run to every site on the internet but God's site, but he will still honor his covenant and will fight for us. "The battle is not yours, but it is the Lord's, but the victory is yours."

Some dark places on earth do not know Christ Jesus. Remember the land of the Chaldeans, where there was no light of the power and knowledge of God. When people are cruel, they are without God in their lives and need to be taught. We should not be afraid of their faces. When people don't have God, they do not have anything to humble themselves for. We see people not submitting or humbling themselves to God or one another. I suggest that they submit to God first. We must show our faithfulness and obligation to God. We must be loyal and constant in love with God and his Word. When we love God and show our devotion to him, he will honor and deliver us and we will find help in time of need.

Why Is My Soul Cast Down and Disquieted?

Our holy love is the life and soul of our relationship with Christ, and we must walk in that love. How does our love walk in Christ Jesus? We must have a thirst for love and keep our minds on things above—the higher life—not the things on earth. "Seek ye first His kingdom and His righteousness and his way of doing and being right and all these other things will be added unto you." We have his Word, his blood, and his name sent from above to deliver and cover us. The name of Jesus Christ is used as a password or secret code and combination to the safe; in our prayers, he connects us to our heavenly Father. We should thirst after the things above and have a strong desire to seek God and praise him. We should want more of God and nobody but God; we don't want guidance from anybody but God, the Spirit in us.

We are living souls; we get no rest until we come to God. Anyone who appreciates God's goodness of a new day should desire to be in the presence of God, who gave it. People with pain and sorrow in their lives long for God's presence.

If you have not been to church in a while, God's presence is what you should be desiring. You may think you have everything you need, but there is something missing in you—Jesus Christ. You miss being thirsty after God, and you want to be in his presence. This is how you will enjoy your prosperity. "In the presence of God there is fullness of joy and pleasures forevermore." The world notices you haven't been going to church lately and wonders what is wrong with you, where God, who is in you, is. You had a seed planted in you when you were saved, but it is dormant. You had the ark of God in you, but it appears that it is not there anymore. You are a walking ark of God, a temple of the almighty God. They think you lost your God, but they are mistaken.

I thank God for being in me, on me, around me, and for me. God is right there where we left him. People think that when they have robbed us of our Bibles, ministers, and assemblies of members, they have robbed us of our God. God gave us all these resources, but he is not in just those resources. He is everywhere; he even works in the likeness of or resemblance of a person or thing. We know where our God is and where to find him. No matter where we are, there is always a way to communicate with him. When God doesn't appear in our lives immediately, we might think he has abandoned us. When we consider the number of churches in the world, it's hard to believe no one has witnessed to some people yet. Delay does not mean denial. People will try to pour salt on our wounds and kick us when we are up as well as when we are down. We must abandon those who intend to play with our hopes and confidence in God. The world and Satan really don't like God in us because we are his image.

When we leave God's presence, we end up like the Prodigal Son in a pigpen with no friends. The Father gives peace to those who love him. We have free access to God's house for our needs because we will be at home in Christ Jesus, and we know how to act when we're at home. We should never let the enemy bring our self-esteem down. When we have God's holy love, he will lead us to our God-ordained destiny. We should have confident expectation in that. The enemy loves to attack us when we are uneasy, disturbed, restless, and anxious. That is when we need to encourage ourselves with our confidence in God. We must take hold of his promises and power and praise him for his help, favor, and support. His love will satisfy us.

Don't murmur or complain; check your thought life and think of things above. Pray to God concerning your sense knowledge. A lot of problems come from sense knowledge. I pray a prayer to conquer my thought life. It takes only a word to conquer a thought, so let your words agree with the Word of God. Take your religion wherever you go. Always keep him in your heart. When you represent God wherever you go, your heart is set on him. God told Moses, "You will be as a God to them."

Something will always come against us until we leave this earth. We may not know what we are doing and where God is leading us, but he does. He has already cleared the way, and he knows that after the storm, the sun will shine in our lives.

Those who are faithful to him will always have his favor. People will say no when God will say yes. Good things will happen in your life, and your bright light will shine in their faces. The spirit inside them is only trying to discourage you. We know that "greater is He that is in me than he that is in the world." Jesus is your rock; he will help you achieve the victory you desire. Gird your loins and keep your mind set on the higher things, not the things of earth. Stop letting your carnal mind operate; hold the thoughts, feelings, and purposes of God's heart. Let's put on the mind of Christ and remember, "As a man thinketh in his heart then so is he."

Satan's Spider Web

Sometimes, we get caught in a transparent spiderweb, something we just didn't see, and others will come after us as if they were spiders and we were bugs. They might try to take advantage of our predicament in many ways. If we had seen the web, we would not have walked into it.

The web could be in your house. It could be your neighbor who is caught in a snare with a bad habit or relationship he complains about just like a bug shaking in a web. We should encourage all brethren. The parable of the good Samaritan tells us how we should treat all others as our neighbors. When we were saved, we became the captain over problems that others might have. Any learning that you receive at church or at home should be applied to that moment or situation. This can happen only if you love your neighbor as yourself. God wants us all to love one another. Once you go through boot camp or a new members' class, you become equipped to pray for those who do not know how to ascend to the throne of God. It just might be people who will not pray for themselves. Don't speak peace to your neighbor and have mischief against them in your heart. We should pray that God will bless our enemies and someday rule their minds and hearts. We should pray that the Holy Spirit will guide them. We can ask the Lord to give them pastors, leaders, and neighbors who will guide them into the wisdom and understanding of his Word. We were born again to help lead them out of their troubles. We should pray and love those who don't care about their souls. We can keep shaking the web, pray, and let God fight our battles. He will free us from traps.

We should encourage others who are caught in traps. The webs of life can catch the best of us and cause us to shake and fight for our lives before the proverbial spider attacks us. Some will escape webs, but others will lose heart and give up trying to get out. Some spiders are poisonous, and some relationships and drugs are poisonous. Some people try to save themselves through therapy while others will stop shaking the web and just die. Suicide rates are high, and some overdose on drugs because they are caught in a web of life.

The fly that shook its way out should remind us that there is hope. Who the Son set free is free indeed. If you die and go to hell, there will be no hope. Remember the battle is not yours but the Lord's. When we are caught in the snares and webs of life, we should keep shaking or speaking the Word of God until we get out. When we are caught in bad circumstances, we should not give up. Just as boldly as we got into it, we should go boldly to the throne of God and speak our way out along with shaking Satan's web. We should first repent because we will know what we did; we should clear the air between us and God.

God will forgive us, and then we can forgive ourselves and get busy living through his Word. "I can do all things through Jesus Christ which strengthens me." Say that you are strong in the Lord, and his might will strengthen you. "Greater is he that is in me than he who is in the world. God did not give me the spirit of fear but of power, and of love and a sound mind." Psalm 35:8–9 says,

> Let destruction come upon him at unawares; and let the net that he hath hid catch himself: into that very destruction let him fall. And my soul shall be joyful in the Lord, it shall rejoice in his salvation.

Cast down every imagination that exalts itself against the true knowledge of God. You are the head and not the tail. You are above, not beneath. "God always causes me to triumph through Christ Jesus." Sometimes, we are caught in traps because of our sin. Maybe it was a sin that we became comfortable in or a presumptuous sin while taking God for granted and our sin found us out. It could be a secret sin, one that goes no further than the heart. Ask God to frustrate the enemy's hand against you. Wherever there is a web, a spider is nearby. If there is a web, somebody spun it. Satan sets traps in our thoughts to keep us from our God-ordained destinies. He comes to steal, kill, and destroy. Just as a fly in a web starts shaking and buzzing, start confessing your sin, repent of your sins of omission known and unknown, and clear the way to the throne of God. Hurry up and get in line with God and his Word. It is better to make your confessions and pray every day. Revenge all disobedience when your freedom or your obedience is fulfilled by saying what God says about it. Don't lose heart, don't faint, and don't give up. If you think you will lose, you have already lost. Success is a matter of willpower.

If we are aware of everything that leads to evil and get rid of all appearances of sin, we will have a better walk with God. We must serve God only and liberally and serve him in the strength of his grace that came from him. The closer we come to everlasting praise, the more we should act and talk the language and do the work of the world we are about to enter. Great consequences depend upon what is innermost and godly in our hearts. We must ask God to give us clean and perfect hearts. Our character shows up in our choices and desires. Solomon asked for wisdom so God's house could be built and to help him lead God's people. God did not give him wisdom so he could brag about it but to help him govern his people righteously. Solomon put God and his Word in first place in his life (2 Chronicles 2:1–10).

We were not born for ourselves but for God and those around us. We must worship together as the angels on the ark facing one another and attending to their worship; that is how we should worship God. We are seated with Christ in heavenly places. We received a kingdom that cannot be moved; let us serve God with reverence and godly fear. We should not worship angels; we should worship with them because we are in communication with them. We must worship God because angels must do the will of God.

Remember the veil that was parted between the temple and the most holy place. We must move forward and come from behind the curtain. Some people still need others to go before God for them. In those days, the worshippers were kept at a distance, but at the death of Christ, the veil was rent, and through him, we are made near to God. Now, we can go boldly to the throne of God and enter the holy of holies. We must live sober and disciplined lives. As we devote ourselves to God, we must keep our eye and our faith on Jesus, who saved us with his blood.

We must keep our focus on Jesus Christ and use the faith given us to help purify our consciences so we can serve God honestly. The Word can cleanse our hearts so we can represent the Father and Jesus well.. James 4:8 (KJV) says, "Draw nigh to God, and He will draw nigh to you. Cleanse your hands ye sinners; and purify your hearts, ye double-minded." We must be careful of our thoughts because they are like words to God. The closer we come to him, the purer we must be. The ark was, just as Christ was, in the presence of God. When we let Christ into our hearts, he becomes the law written in our hearts. We become arks of the covenant, temples of the Holy Spirit.

God gave us power because he took into consideration our weaknesses and infirmities. God reveals himself to those who can bear his power. He even put words in simple forms as parables to open people's minds. Jesus showed us how to take over Satan's palace. Everything that is not Christlike must come out so that rightful owner can take possession. Let the rightful owner who is Christ Jesus come in and drop that zero Satan, who kidnapped humankind in the garden of Eden. We desire to have God in our hearts, and we must make room so we can accommodate him.

Praise and worship bring the presence of God. Worshipping God is the subject of the gospel because this is what we will do for eternity—praise God. When we let God work in us, we are giving him praise by accommodating him and giving him the glory due him. Worshipping the kingdom of grace helps make us holy. This is when God's glory will shine in the house of God.

Worshippers are discoverers of the goodness of God as he reveals his mind and himself to them. During the process, God gives strength to his people and will protect them against all evil. God will give them sufficiency in all things so they will abound in every good work and charitable donation. God blesses us with peace. It is hard to be at peace when our bills are not paid, but Jesus brought us peace, and we must keep it in the right perspective and appreciate it. Peace is God's plan for all people. "And the chastisement of our peace was upon Him and with His stripes we are healed."

I had the opportunity to evangelize with one of the greatest teams next to the twelve disciples of Jesus Christ. Almost every one of us branched out in different parts of Memphis. We witnessed on the streets showing God's power by showing signs and wonders, and we brought people to Christ. It was another way of giving God praise. Shall the dust praise thee? Praising God can turn your mourning into dancing. Psalm 30:12 says, "To the end that my glory may sing praise to thee, and not be silent. O Lord my God, I will give thanks unto thee forever." When our spirits are separated at death from our bodies, they will return to God. We will still be praising him, but our bodies, which will go back to the earth, will not be able to praise him. We need to let our complaints turn into praise. We must keep ourselves in praise mode to God so we will have his guidance. We should pray for his direction and water it with praise. We should be like David and commit our spirits to the Lord. Psalm 31:5 reminds us, "Into thine hand I commit my spirit: thou hast redeemed me, O Lord of truth."

Our souls and spirits are our most important assets. When afflictions come upon us, concern for our souls increases. When the cares of the world hit us hard, we tend to forget our souls and become our own gods. Our souls are the only thing we really own. We may be able to lose our car or house, but we should put more value on our eternal souls and spirits. Luke 21:19 says, "In your patience possess ye your soul." The most important thing we can do is commit our souls into the hands of God and let his will be done in our lives on earth as it is in heaven.

People will try to rob us of our money and reputations, but we shouldn't let them rob us of the peace of the Lord. He knows the exact time to deliver us, and we must wait patiently until then. In 1 Samuel 24:4, David told his men that the time had not yet come for his deliverance from Saul because it would be sin. We jump in front of God's timing and sin if we try to help ourselves out of situations and become our own gods. We end up doing life in prison trying to do it ourselves. We should always wait on God because he has his own way of delivering his people. If we don't receive what God has laid up for us in his promises and covenant, it will be due to our doubt or unbelief. When our faith falls short, it doesn't mean God's promises did because they are yes and amen.

Therefore, we should love the Lord, keep our consciences clear from sin, repent, and have pure hearts toward God. We should be strong in the Lord and in the power of his might having a good heart knowing that he is on our side. Trusting in God will give us the help we need from dangers seen and unseen and will strengthen our hearts. He will show us his favor because he loves to have our hearts pursue him. The sacrifice of praise pleases the Lord better than oxen or bulls or money. Where there is unity, the Lord commands the blessing. God's goodness is his glory, and he just loves it when we give him the glory of it (Psalm 19:31). Unite your spirit with the almighty God and receive the blessing.

According to 2 Chronicles 6:24–28, God knows the heart, and trouble will bring most people to God including those who usually would not give him the time of day. When they come, we must get them to repent of their sin and let them know that the kingdom of heaven is at hand. God knows our hearts. He is a discerner of our thoughts and intents. God knows our hearts so well that he knows how many beats they make. God has experience with his creation from Genesis all the way through the New Testament.

God discovered that there was no such thing as a sinless man; he sent Jesus to atone for our sin. He delivered the Israelites to their enemies many times because of their disobedience. The forgiveness of our sins will make a way for all the answers to our prayers.

God returns his mercy and goodness to us when we have repented of our sin and turned from them to seek him. When we pray, it takes possession of our temple and it gives us rest. What and who can do more for us than God, who created us? God's spirit in me strengthens me. Even the doctors told me when I was paralyzed that they had done all they could for me and that it was between me and the Lord. It has been me and the Lord ever since that day because it showed me that without God, I could do nothing. I like the way he catches me when I begin to fall.

We are in the soul business, and God wants to make us a public blessing to bring his creation back to him to have fellowship with him. God wants us saved so we can save others and our temples can bear fruit. When our spirits are sanctified, they will be on fire to witness to others. The fire will burn up everything that was not right in our hearts. We need to keep this fire burning at the altar of our hearts and stay humble in the presence of God.

We must expect trouble when we witness to others. In 2 Chronicles 14:1–8, King Asa expected trouble in his time of peace and fortified the cities and put walls and gates up. When we are witnessing, we must be combat ready. Our adversary roams around seeking whom he might devour, so we have to be alert and awake. In 1 Thessalonians 5:16 (AMP), we read,

> Behold the bridegroom cometh, but as to the suitable times and the precise season, and dates, brethren you have no necessity for anything being written to you, for you yourselves know perfectly well that the day of the return of the Lord will come as unexpecting, and suddenly as a thiefinthenight.

Destruction, ruin, and death will come upon those who think all is well as suddenly as labor pains come upon a woman with child, but we are not in darkness for that to take us by surprise; we are the sons and daughters of light and day. Let us not sleep as the rest do; let us keep wide awake, alert, and watchful. When we are ready, we are quick to act and serve God. We are waiting and willing to be used. Those who drowned in Noah's days were caught off guard. Instead of God sending floods to destroy us, he will send floods of his favor to us.

We are in a struggle against the enemy. We must bravely resist him as combatants. We fight our way through to warn people about the truth and expose the lies of the enemy. We declare the whole counsel of God and point out the enemy's dangers. We pull people out of burning buildings and away from other dangers including diseases. We tell others about Jesus, the medicine that they should take. We should always be ready and be strong for our work will be well rewarded.

CHAPTER 5

Social Awareness

What Is Religion?

> Religion is seeking God and enquiring after Him. Applying ourselves to him upon all occasions and giving reverence in everything we do. To resolve to end one's immoral behavior, A set of beliefs, values and practice based on the teaching of a spiritual leader (Jehovah God in this case). A system grounded in such belief and worship, the life or condition of a person in a religious order, Belief in and reverence for a supernatural power regarded as creator and governor of the universe.

If you seek him, you will find him, but if you forsake God and his ordinances, he will forsake you. The Lord is with you all the while you are with him. Even when you leave him, he will not forsake you because of his grace. You do not deserve his grace, but he has his arms wide open just ready to love you because he is love. You are his creation, and he want your communion. Others will forsake you, but God will not.

I made God my habitation by giving him my praise. God inhabits the praises of his people. I spend my days hanging out with God because he is my confidence by faith and prayer. When I am with the Lord, I have assurance that he will never let me fall. No other power is greater than the Lord. Cast me not off now in the time of my old age, forsake me not when my strength fails. My strength fails where there was strength of body and vigor of mind, strong sight, and strong limbs. When we quit when problems in life overtake us, we have the appearance of a person who doesn't know God.

Psalm 71 says that you must put your confidence in God and make your professions of that confidence. If you do, you will never be disappointed. Let your experiences and victories encourage you. God watched over you when you were not able to take care of yourself. God held you up and led you to a safe place in him. Have confidence that he will not let you fall now. I, Steven Treadwell, thank you, Father God, for helping me when I could not help myself. My confidence and hope are in you, Father God, that you will not abandon me now because I am as helpless now as I was when I was paralyzed.

I will always praise you, Lord God. I always fear you especially in times of old age and when my strength fails me. David said, "Be not far from me in this confidence." He prayed, "Make hast to my help before I perish before help come."

The adversaries of my soul do not want to repent, so let them be confounded into everlasting shame. Let my enemies say what they will, but I will hope continually in the darkest and cloudiest days. I will hope till the end. My heart is established in faith. I hope I am in your strength, and I will not sit down in despair; I will encourage myself and move forward. By the strength of your grace, I stay hopeful in you. I pray to leave my testimony about you to succeeding generations in power with pleasure and giving the advantage of religion and the truth of God's promises. Our lack of reverence for God and lack of duty as parents when children disrespect us are irreligious and irregular (Psalm 71).

When followers of Christ go through the hypocrite process and fall away, they look just like the world. They do the same thing as those who do not know God or his ways. They become hostile to or seem indifferent to religion. They take on the enemy's character. They display their enmity and end up in hostile environments. We must control our thoughts and not let our emotions run our thought life.

Ask the Lord how to number your days. Ask God to give you wisdom and grace. Death will be the end of all the trials and tests of your character and the end of your ability to meet the requirements for heaven. All the joys of the wicked will cease, and it will be the end of all the righteous grief.

One of Satan's biggest tricks is to make us think we have more time than we do. We start to put things off until later thinking we will be able to get back to them. There were some things I wanted to do with my brother, Richard, and my best friend, Johnny Woodhouse, but they died suddenly, and I did not get the chance. When we consider how short life is, we will be concerned about doing all we can while we can. We begin to do it with all our might. James 4:14 says, "Where ye know not what shall be on the morrow. For what is your life? It is even a vapor, that appeared for a little time, and then vanished away." The little time we live is nothing compared to God's eternity. The next life will be eternal. We need the wisdom of God to live our days on earth to assist us in our new man or spirit that we received from God.

We are here for a minute and then disappear. Our days are uncertain; the only sure thing we have is our spirit from God, which will return to him. In Psalm 23, David said that God was his shepherd who would not let him want for anything. We are in God's pasture and receive all the comforts of this life from his hand. We receive our daily bread from him—every word that proceeds out of his mouth. God makes us to lie down in quietness and contentment in whatever state we are in. We learn how to be abased and keep our souls at ease in him.

When we believe God and receive his Word, he shows us the way to walk in him in love and with a good heart. God feeds us and refreshes us every morning with new mercies. In his presence are eternal pleasures. He leads us to peaceful waters that agree with peaceful spirits. God put us in right standing with himself when Jesus died on the cross and rose from the dead. He leads us in the path of righteousness for his name's sake. He led me to my job that he prepared specifically for me—writing this book. The systemized knowledge derived from his observation, study, and experimentation he carried out in the garden of Eden after the fall of man was to determine the nature of his creation. God's way is the best way for humankind. We cannot walk in God's path unless he leads us.

He restores my soul when I fall from grace and when I cry with the Holy Spirit. I dropped the ball like David when he had Uriah killed after getting Bathsheba pregnant. Nathan was sent to tell him, "Thou art the man." God restored David's soul. God may allow us to fall into sin, but he will not let us wallow in filth as the Prodigal Son did. I have received God's goodness all my life and will never distrust him no matter what comes my way. If I have lost limbs or hands, I walk through the valley of the shadow of death. When I was paralyzed, I did not have any arms or legs. I had to humble myself to everyone who came into the room. That was when I learned humility to God and others because without God, I could do nothing. I even needed help urinating and could not at that time wipe my butt. Don't let the shadows of your past take the shine out of your future. Though I am near death during danger, I pull my book of Job up deep in the valley. I will be easy like Sunday morning. What would give me strength is knowing that it is only the shadow of death, which has no evil in it; it is a roaring lion that will not hurt you. Satan has a valley of shadows that bring fear to God's people to destroy their peace. Death is only a step away, but we just step right into it safely to the other side. There is no evil in it for a child of God. When I was paralyzed, I was just glad to be alive. Death cannot separate us from God's love. Death can kill the body but not the soul. We have a good shepherd who will lead us through the valley—Jesus.

God's presence comforts us. The shepherd's crook gathers the saints as well as those who stray from him and drives away sinners. His mercy prepares a table for us with all we need including eternity with him. He anoints us with oil. We shall not want. His goodness and mercy will follow us all the days of our lives. God will love us all the way, and we must trust and believe in him all the way. When his goodness and mercy follow us, we will dwell in the house of the Lord forever.

When trouble comes, it will drive you to God. The distressing and difficult circumstances we find ourselves in put us in situations that only God can get us out of. Most of the time, sin was the cause or source of the distress. Sin brings disturbance to the peace we have in God and makes life difficult. After Adam and Eve sinned, their lives became hard; they had to work for what they had already had as a gift from God in the garden. People today want everything instantly just as Adam and Eve did.

Cain slew Abel and brought on public unrest. Our society is at unrest even as I speak with record number of murders every year. The blood of all these killings is crying out to God. The disorder that came at the Tower of Babel is a problem today. Races are not satisfied with government passing sinful laws that citizens don't agree with. Sin afflicts us with pain and discomfort. Jesus came as a troubleshooter or mediator to investigate the condition of our hearts. Trouble will drive you to God, but you will not find it vain to seek him.

We trust God when there is nothing else to trust. God has all our hearts in his hand, and he turns them however he pleases. Satan is a deceiver, and now we can see how one lying spirit can make four hundred lying prophets. We must hold onto God's counsel. Those who cannot be counseled cannot be helped. Our young need wise and good instruction because it is so easy for them to get off track as Adam and Eve had. God left them to themselves for a moment, and now look at his creation. It is easier for us to build temples than to be temples of God. We have altars in our hearts, and we are living sacrifices.

Chronicles 24:15–26 (KJV) shows us that we must hear God speak and that we must resemble him. They went to church and heard the word in verse 18 but went out of church "serving groves and idols and wrath came upon Judah and Jerusalem for their trespasses." Carnal Christians leave services praising God, but then they change the station back to the world. Sometimes, they leave church fighting or arguing with one another. Verse 20 shows us how God speaks through his prophets.

> And the spirit of the God came upon Zechariah the son of Jehoiada the priest, which stood above the people, and said unto them, thus said God, why transgress ye the commandments of the Lord, that ye cannot prosper? Because ye have forsaken the Lord, he hath forsaken you.

We need to make God our friend because many people shed tears in their troubles but do not get rid of their sin. Sin is the root of their problems. God will not throw his church aside. He corrects his servants by sending them into fiery furnaces not to torment them but to purify them. If we seek God, we will prosper. He will help us until we become strong. He will guide us unless we get lifted in pride.

Walk with him in humility and prayer so when he turns his head for a moment and leaves you to test you, you will past the test. When you go to the throne room of grace, give him your majesty time to bless you. It will be just like leaving church before the benediction because you may miss the final blessing.

In 1 Peter 2:1–5, we learn how to stop evil speaking and to desire the milk of the Word. We taste God's goodness. We are living stones of a spiritual house and a holy priesthood.

Angels

We must activate our faith so that the angels will help us. In Luke 1:26–28, the angel Gabriel was sent from God with a message. There is agreement and unity in the kingdom of God where he alone receives blessings and honor. Satan wants to tear down our unity with the Father and the Son. Seals can be opened only by Christ, and God commissions the angels to carry out his Word. We must fast and pray God's Word back to him unceasingly. Daniel 10:10–13 tells us how angels hear and talk to us.

> And behold, a hand touched me, which set me upon my knees and upon the palms of my hands. And he said unto me, O Daniel, a man greatly beloved, understand the words that I speak unto thee, and stand upright: for unto thee am I now sent. And when he had spoken this word unto me, I stood trembling. Then said he unto me, Fear not, Daniel: for from the first day that thou didst set thine heart to understand, and to chasten thyself before thy God, thy words were heard, and I am come for thy words. But the prince of the kingdom of Persia withstood me one and twenty days: but lo, Michael, one of the chief princes, came to help me; and I remained there with the kings of Persia. Now I am come to make thee understand what shall befall thy people in the latter days: for yet the vision is for many days.

There are different types of angels. In Isaiah 6:2, we read, "Above it stood the seraphim's: each one had six wings; with twain he covered his face, and with twain he covered his feet, and with twain he did fly."

God sent Gabriel in Luke 1:26–28.

> And in the sixed month the angel Gabriel was sent from God unto a city of Galilee Named Nazareth. To a virgin espoused to a man whose name was Joseph, of the house of David; and the virgin's name was Mary. And the Angel came in unto her, and said, hail thou that art highly favored, the Lord are with thee: blessed art thou among women.

Daniel 6:22 tells us how God sent an angel to shut the lion's mouth. God sent angels to give us encouragement in Genesis 16:7–11, when the angel talked with Hagar, Sarai's maid. God used his angels for guidance in Exodus 14:19: "There are angels also to shield us." "And the Angel of God, which went before the camp of Israel, removed and went behind them; and the pillar of the cloud went from before their face, and stood behind them." That's right. Angels have our back. They are God's swift messengers.

God will also punish with his angels as he did in 2 Samuel 24:16.

> And when the angel stretched out his hand upon Jerusalem to destroy it, the Lord repented him of the evil, and said to the angel that destroyed the people, it is enough: stay now thine hand. And the angel of the Lord was by the threshing place of Araunah the Jebusite.

Angels patrol the earth as they did in 2 Kings 6:16–18, when Elisha told the young man, "And he answered, fear not for they that be with us is more than they that be with them." One angel fed Elijah when he ran from Jezebel and encouraged him to eat and get some rest. Angels will destroy evil. Revelation 20:1–3 reads,

And I saw an angel come down from heaven, having the key of the bottomless pit and a great chain in his hand. And laid hold on the dragon, that old serpent, which is the devil, and Satan, and bound him a thousand years, And cast him into the bottomless pit, and shut him up, and set a seal upon him, that he should deceive the nations no more, till the thousand years should be fulfilled: and after that he must be loosed a little season.

When we speak the Word of God in faith, angels are released to bring it to pass. I had my experience with an angel priest that came to my house along with two cherubim. I was taken up in spirit as I looked back and vanished in the air.

Monsters of Our Imagination

Evil is being intensified, and "curses are chasing sinners while blessings chase the righteous" (Proverbs 13:21 LB). The truth will be standing tall after all the lies have been told and exposed. Our sin will find us out. A lot of people are jumping on the lie train—any way of living contrary to the Word of God. We need to get all the advice that we can for the rest of our lives (Proverbs 19:20). We must pray to the Lord to let the plans of the rebellious people boomerang back at them and let them step into their own traps. We must stay with God no matter what Satan throws at us. The protection God gives us should motivate us to commit to him. We must behave valiantly and not think of ourselves more highly than we should. We must take charge of our emotions and not let them take charge of us. We are to stay away from fear and sense knowledge. What something looks like, feels like, taste like, or sounds like is sense knowledge, the source of all our pressures. We have faith, courage, and prayer when we depend on God but fear, confusion, and pressure when we depend on others. Our condition on earth is due to whatever mental condition we might have. We can be in pleasure or in fear and grief. The images in our minds are only the terrifying monsters of our imagination.

I was watching TV and saw some same-sex kissing. It was a subliminal suggestion. Our conscious minds work when we are awake, but our subconscious minds are always active. Subliminal messages go past the filtering mechanism of the conscious mind and enter our subconscious minds. Hallucinations are the perception of having seen, heard, touched, or smelled something that wasn't there, figments of our imaginations.

TV commercials of juicy hamburgers can make us crave one. Commercials guide black women to white men. The seeds planted in our minds daily are meant to manipulate society. They are illusions and delusions that we add to make us happy or make us afraid. Some people love monster movies. Some people love to breathe danger. When these dangers materialize in their lives, they are terrified. Things that we go through along with the pains they bring are nothing but vanity.

People dream about becoming rich and therefore at peace, but true peace can be found only in God. All things are uncertain except our being reunited with God, where we originated. Blessed are they who do not lose faith when they are tempted by sex, alcohol, drugs and other sins including witchcraft. God has a great passion for his creation, but he hates sin.

God wants us to have stability as we strive to enter his kingdom. He hates to see his creations running around like unsaved beasts. He wants to provide for us so we can rest as he did and see that it is good. We were born by the Word, and we must be nourished by the Word, our manna from heaven, our spiritual food. If we let God's Word have first place in our lives, it will guide us and accomplish what it was sent out to do. Our new mercies should put us in mind of our former mercies.

God will put things in our hearts to do what we would not have done normally. He puts things in our heads for his purpose and plan for our lives. God gives us the grace in the things that pertain to life and godliness. The book of James tells us that every perfect gift is from above. If any good things appear from our or others' hearts, we must assume that God put them there.

This should give us confidence in our prayer life like Nehemiah had. He approached God with a holy confidence. He told God in chapter 1, verse 6,

> Let thine ear now be attentive, and thine eyes open, that thou mayest hear the prayer of thy servant, which I pray before thee now, day and night, for the children of Israel

91

> thy servants, and confess the sins of the children of Israel, which we have sinned against thee: both I and my father's house have sinned.

I say this prayer for my family. We get our best pleas in prayer from God's promises. I must be in devotion to God. I show my affection to God by confessing my sin and forgiving those who sin against me. I am a sinner, but I don't go back to my bondage, my Egypt.

Ezra's prayer to God came in humility after making a great trespass in Ezra 9:7 (KJV).

> Since the days of our fathers have we been in great trespass unto this day: and for our iniquities have we, our kings, and our priest has been delivered into the hand of the king, of the lands, to sword to captivity, and to a spoil, and to confusion of face, as it is this day.

We need to say, "Lord teach me and remove all the thoughts of foolishness that is sin out of our minds and hearts." Malachi 3:16 (AMP) tells us, "Those who feared the Lord talked often one to another, and the Lord listen and heard it, and a book of remembrance was written before Him of those who reverenced and worshipfully feared the Lord and thought on His name."

Self-Evaluation

If everyone swept around his or her front door, the streets would be clean. If every Christian brought just one soul to Christ, we would all be saved and we would all have done our duty.

Stay close to God's divine protection and you will succeed. Satan wants to hinder your purpose. Stay close and plugged in to God and it! Whatever it is will come to pass. "Yes, we will revive the stones that are now rubbish which are burned" (Nehemiah 4:2 KJV). Keep close to the soul business with the sword of the Word. If you have the mind of Christ and hold the thoughts, feelings, and purpose of his heart and if God is thinking on you, you will have enough. We should hate sin and be afraid of God; he said in Revelation 3:16, "Because thou art lukewarm, and neither cold nor hot, I will sue thee out of my mouth."

Nehemiah walled the city in faith. He kept his eye on the promise of replenishing. We must keep our service to God and pray to him, praise him, and preach his Word. Wherever we go, we are to serve him. Darkness and trouble can come to us when we are doing God's will, but we must remember that the greater one is in us. Wherever the darkness or ignorance of others begins is where our pulpits should stand. Our pulpits are wherever we stand for the Word of God.

We must show others their sin because this is what is wounding their character. Sin shows their misery, and they don't see the dangers of their sin. We should not let sin drive us from God; we should run to him, our source, our resource, and our strength. We must put on the garment of praise, not the spirit of heaviness. The joy of the Lord is my strength. Holy joy flows with us in our obedience. We look good to ourselves when we look in the mirror of the Word and see that everything that was torn apart has been repaired in our lives. When we were in sin, it had us in poverty and slavery. This is what brought us into all our problems.

We need conversion from the course of the world to the Word of God. "Those that forsake the worship of God forsake God." God said, "Be ye holy for I am holy." Some people say it doesn't take all that, but I believe they are shy of living holy because it conflicts with the little gods they serve, those that they keep hidden. They fear persecution and reproach that comes with holiness and want to blend in with the world. When we get into a relationship with God, we must not commit adultery by worshipping other gods or being unequally yoked with nonbelievers. We are living temples, and we must throw out anything that generates sin. When we repent of our sin, it is replaced by confessing with the mouth and believing in the heart, and the blood of Jesus is applied to it with faith. Then we are kept by the grace of God's spirit for every good work. When we work to no purpose at all, it becomes vainglory (Esther 1:1–9).

Tell People How You Escaped

We should all be messengers to others about the gospel of Jesus Christ and how we became God's children after we rebuked sin: "I only am escaped alone to tell thee" (Job 1:15 KJV). We were left to tell the news, and sometimes it may be bad news, but we must tell it to others to help them in their situations. Think twice about what you are to say and speak once. We don't want to be like Job's friends playing God and passing judgment. After we get saved, we should work as the angels do because we are God's servants too. We should be waiting to hear from God, and we should be working servants. Angels are immortal and pure while we are mortal, but we still must do as the angels do and fix our hearts.

Our wisdom is no match for God's wisdom. We are frail and sinful and on our way to the grave. How can we be more just than God is? Our consciences must be awakened when God gives us our burning bush experience or our Damascus road experience. God informs us of our duty. We know that God does great things because there is nothing too hard for him to do. He can tell us all we need to know by his counsel and his Word. God does great things for us, and his purpose will not be fulfilled until the end of our time. God will exalt the humble, the lowly in heart, and he will comfort us. Isaiah 33:16 says, "He shall dwell on high: his place of defense shall be the munitions of rocks; bread shall be given him; his waters shall be sure." We must not give into despair. Some things in life are bad for some but encouragement for others. This is when we should hope the best in the worst of times. God will get the glory when he sends help to the helpless and hope to the hopeless.

When we make God's truth look good by living it, we will have peace with God and become friends with him. God wants us to have the peace of Christ through his Word. He will place us on a solid foundation. Sometimes, it is not enough to just hear the truth; we should be made wiser and better by it. We should honor, magnify, and stay in communion with him always. He can break the power of sin and our will to sin. He breaks every yoke. Though our beginnings may have been small and we may have just a little cruet of oil, we should stay on course and we will see good days and God's blessing shall multiply and bring an increase. God gives us his grace and comforts us.

God's Secret Enemy—The Hypocrite

The hypocrite's hope was built around lies he told himself and started believing. Most people fall back into the world because of riches and worldly possessions. Hypocrites use money as an excuse to sin. God's enemy goes to church but is very disobedient to him. He chooses to sin because he always needs more. Instead of waiting on God, he decides to be his own god. Comparing his life with others and looking at what he has, the hypocrite decides to abort God's mission. He builds his confidence because the grass looks greener on the other side. He doesn't know that the grass is light, hallowed, and empty. Money gotten by sin is usually spent on more sin, and the money withers quickly. This is the path of those who forget God; the hypocrite's hope begins to perish.

The hypocrite has its own imagination about Christianity. He has a high opinion of his abilities and worth. He feels he should be able to live in comfort like anyone else. His thoughts become his reality, and he feels it should be acceptable to all. He is only showing his disbelief. The end is coming, and this is a sign of the end-time. Many oppose the kingdom of God. There will be some seducers called Antichrists among us. They don't have communion with us anymore. "For, if they had been of us, they would have continued with us" (1 John 2:19).

The Israelites brought rebuke on themselves by dealing treacherously with God. He had strengthened them, but they turned back in the day of battle. They were defeated by the Philistines during Eli's time (1 Samuel 4:10–11) when the ark was taken prisoner, but David brought it back. Sin subtracts from people and takes away their hearts from God. They forget his works and wonders. When we disobey God, we forget his goodness.

When we are saved but become backsliders or hypocrites, we put ourselves in danger. Numbers 14:22 shows us how God's chosen people provoked God ten times in the wilderness. As Israel did, we forget his former favors. Hypocrites should look at their notes to see how many times God went to bat for them before they backslid. When hypocrites backslide, they leave God altogether. We should never forget what God brought us through. God sent angels among them to do evil unto them. They were decoying angels or angels of punishment. He smote all the firstborn when they made it to Canaan. Their children were like their fathers and brought their old behavior into the Promised Land like some people in the church bring their old behavior and will not let the old man die. God never leaves us, but we leave him. When hypocrites or backsliders leave God, they become easy targets for the enemy. God permitted the Philistines to take the ark prisoner like a first-place prize. This showed that God had forsaken not only the tabernacle but also the ark.

God delivered his strength into captivity. This is the same way Christians deliver their strength when they don't know how to use the keys God gave them. It disgraces God when Christians are weakened and overcome. When we abandon God, we make it look as if the enemy has won. Even Hophni and Phineas were killed by the sword. They flipped the script on God and sinned before him. Then David erected a tent for the ark after he recaptured it. Christians receive their rewards from God using his Word, but hypocrites build on their own concerns and beliefs. They put God on the same level as themselves as if God doesn't know what he is talking about. They are proud of their successes and make them their gods. They should know that money fly away. "God resist the proud, but He gives grace unto the humble."

The hypocrite thinks himself secure when he could fall at any time. He becomes insolent and disrespectful in his speech to God. The hypocrite did not understand that God will cut down an upright man. He may be cast down for a period but not cast away. God leaves the wicked to die in their trouble if there is no repentance. The house of the wicked will be brought down eventually.

Those who keep on sinning oppose God. They keep on sinning maybe because they have never really known God. Satan sinned and kept on sinning. Whoever dwells with God is in the safety zone. God makes the wicked's prosperity short. "It is the blessing of the Lord that maketh rich and added no sorrow." Don't be a counterfeit and risk falling.

God Made Us and Not We Ourselves

> So, God created man in His own image … And the Lord God formed man of the dust of the ground and breathed into his nostrils the breath of life; and man became a living soul. (Genesis 1:27, 2:7 KJV)

The soul is what animates the body; it is a gift from God along with the mind, the will, and emotions. We must make sure our thoughts agree with God's will so our plans will succeed. Keeping our emotions intact helps us stay on the right path with God. We do not want to be moved out of position by letting the enemy get us upset; that will take us from our destiny, not to it. Good choices will keep us in the will of God, but bad choices will drive us from God's will for our lives. One bad choice can start the dominoes falling and send us in a direction we didn't want to go. We should control our emotions and not get played out of position. Our bones, muscles, and tendons protect what is inside our bodies including our hearts and lungs. Our bodies were structured with the wisdom, power, and the goodness of God, who gave us life. The wisdom of God is so far out of our reach that we can't begin to know his structure. What is hidden of God is much more than what we can see. The nature of God is beyond our ability to understand.

We find God when we search for him. Acts 17:27–28 says,

> That they should seek the Lord, if haply they might feel after him, and find Him, though He be not far from every-one of us. For in Him we live and move and have our being; as certain also of your own poets have said, "For we are His offspring."

God gave man everything he needed, but man's sin trashed all those gifts. We know that God is, but we don't know what he looks like. We do know that

> God is spirit and those who worship Him must worship Him in spirit and in truth. God gives us wisdom so we can even know what is the breadth, the length, and depth, and height; And to know the love of Christ, which passes knowledge, that ye might be filled with all the fullness of God. Now unto Him that is able to do exceeding abundantly above all that we ask or think, according to the power that works in us. (Ephesians 3:17–20)

Obedience is what you are afraid of because of your lack of understanding what God is trying to do in your life. Man thinks he is so smart that he can buy his way out of death. This world's wisdom must die, and he must receive the wisdom of God.

When you die, you will not be able to change anything. Look at the next funeral procession going down the street and realize you could be next. Don't think that you are the only one God could have used. That's right; God wants to use the body he formed from the dust and breathed life into to make you a living soul. Appreciate that God wants to use you because he could have used someone else.

It is our duty to delight ourselves in the Lord and know him. We should love God with all our mind, body, soul, and might. Everything we do should be to please God and be pleased in him. When we trust in the Lord with all our hearts and follow his guidance, he will direct our path. We must acknowledge him in all our ways and commit ourselves to him. We should ask God what to do in every situation and trust that he will bring it to pass. When we rely on his wisdom and promises, he will bring forth our righteousness as the light and our judgment as the noonday.

"The steps of a good man are ordered by the Lord," and God will make a good man look good. He has a good man's back. Keep a good conscience and "cast all your cares on Him for He careth for you." Don't worry, fret, or have anxiety about anything because God's got your back. Just stay submissive to God and humble yourself to him.

When we get saved, we must go in a different direction than the sinful ways of our past. Those who sin will reap and receive their wages and harvest of death. When we have only a little money, we should remember that it could be more than those who have millions. Proverbs 15:16–17 states, "Better is little with the fear of the Lord than great treasure and trouble there with. Better is a dinner of herbs where love is than a stalled ox and hatred there with."

We depend on the Lord and wait while expecting his goodness. Jesus said, "Blessed are the meek for they shall inherent the earth" (Matthew 5:5). God promised the meek a peace that the world couldn't give them. Jesus died on the cross so we would have peace. John 14:27 describes that peace: "Peace I leave with you, my peace I give unto you: not as the world giveth, give I unto you. Let not your heart be troubled, neither let it be afraid." When we pay all that we owe to God, our consciences will be clear. As men of righteousness, we become mirrors of God's kingdom.

When we leave our sins, we need to get serious with God. We must magnify Christ with our words. When we speak God's Word, he works in and through us. "We will have words of love words of life that will produce good things into our lives and the lives of others." Out of the abundance of the heart the mouth speaks. Let it speak God's wisdom. This will make our wills subject to God's will. God's Word should be written on the tablets of our hearts and represent the Father and Jesus well. The love of God will be shed abroad in our hearts and bring his blessings into our lives. We must let the Holy Spirit guide us to all truths and to where our treasures are. We should let God receive glory by making our lives prosperous.

God will keep us from falling into destruction if we stay plugged in to him. If we lose the joy of God's salvation, he will restore it. There will be quiet after the storm and spring after the winter. We must endure those hard seasons in our lives. God gives us sufficiency in all things that we may abound in every good work. God will not leave us to our adversaries. We must wait on him and be steady in his way.

Stay out of sinful situations and even the appearance of sin. Keep your conscience clear and avoid the condemnation of sin. God is good all the time to those who magnify him. When you keep God's way, you will inherent the good land. He will keep you safe and happy because you trust in him.

Why Do We Need God in Our Lives?

We need God's help to understand why we were born. We must give God the glory due him. We need the knowledge of God to know who our source and resource is so we can know where and how to receive what we need. We are his children, and we need to be taught what is right and wrong so the enemy does not lead us astray. Daniel 8:23–27 reads,

> And in the latter times of their times of their kingdom, when the transgressors are come to the full, a king of fierce anger countenance, and understanding dark sentences, shall stand up. And his power shall be mighty, but not by his own power: and he shall destroy wonderfully, and shall prosper, and practice, and shall destroy the mighty and

the holy people. And though his policy also he shall cause craft to prosper in his hand; and he shall magnify himself in his heart, and by peace shall destroy many: he shall also stand up against the Prince of princes; but he shall be broken without hand. And the vision of the evening and the morning which was told is true: wherefore shut thou up the vision; for it shall be for many days. And I Daniel fainted, and was sick certain days; afterwards I rose up and did the kings business; and I was astonished at the vision, but none understood it.

We also must understand hard sentences. Daniel 5:12, 14 says,

Forasmuch as an excellent spirit, and knowledge, and understanding, interpreting of dreams, and showing of hard sentences, and dissolving of doubts, were found in the same Daniel, whom the king named Belteshazzar: now let Daniel be called, and he will show the interpretation … I have even heard of thee, that the spirit of the gods is in thee, and that light and understanding and excellent wisdom is found in thee.

Proverbs 1:6 says, "To understand a proverb, and the interpretation; the words of the wise, the dark saying." God's spirit teaches us to divine sentences so we can discern their meaning. God gave us pastors and leaders that he trusts to lead his people with his Word. God gave us the Bible so we could agree with him on our own. We should assemble so we can encourage one another along our Christian path.

Prayer

Father God I desire to receive wisdom and discipline. I ask for the ability to understand words of insight, by your grace I am acquiring a discipline and prudent life doing what is right, just, and fair. Thank you for giving me prudence, knowledge and discretion. As a wise person I listen and add to my learning, and as a discerning person

I accept guidance so that I may be able to steer my course rightly. Thank you, Father, that I understand Proverbs, parables, the sayings and the riddles of the wise, in the name of Jesus Christ Amen.

Mental Therapy
Now Faith Is …

Now that we have God's Word called his will and his wisdom, let's begin to walk by faith. Faith words spoken by God brought our world into existence. Faith is a spiritual force. Here are the laws of receiving by faith to change things by faith. Hebrews 11:1, "Now faith is the substance of things hoped for and the evidence of things not seen," is a spiritual law we must abide in to receive the things we hope for. In 1 Corinthians 13:13 (KJV), we read, "And now abideth faith, hope, charity, these three, but the greatest is charity." Whatever God spoke, it became.

God created all things by his Word. When we speak God's Word in faith, we must remember that faith is always now. Faith and hope work together because faith is now and hope is in the future. Philippians 1:20 (KJV) says, "According to my earnest expectation and my hope, that in nothing I shall be ashamed, but that with all boldness as always, so now also Christ shall be magnified in my body, whether it be by life, or by death." When we are earnest, we are anxious and persistent in our expectations. We must also be confident in what we are believing God for will come to pass. If we don't apply faith to what we are believing, the substancewillnotmaterialize.

God has goodness waiting for us, and faith is how we call it to ourselves from the future. If we quit using our faith, that means we no longer have real hope. Hope is transferred from the spiritual realm into the natural. We must see ourselves with it and confess with our mouths and believe in our hearts. We should say, "It's mine now! I receive it now!" Don't get impatient and leave the now. Don't let Satan talk you out of the now because you might think what you are believing for is not coming to pass. Hope is earnest, tense, favorable, and confident expectation. The Word of God is the source of all hope. "Hope deferred maketh the heartsick: but when the desire cometh, it is a tree of life" (Proverbs 13:12). If you drop the ball in your faith walk, bounce back every time and remember what had you on fire at first. Faith comes by hearing.

Jesus said in Mark 11:24, "Therefore I say unto you. What things so ever ye desire when ye pray, believe that ye receive them, and ye shall have them." God has all the love and goodness we need and want when we believe we can receive it. We have to walk by faith and practice faith. Our faith comes by hearing the Word of God. We are not moved by what we see or hear because we go by what we know about the integrity of God's Word. Therefore, we don't fret about anything.

Don't let your emotions rule you. Don't let anything pull you back into the flesh or the natural. Walk in the spirit and you will not fulfill the desires of the flesh. Start praise and worship to water what you are believing God for. Praise and thank him on credit. Thank him in advance just for being God.

Praise your way into his presence thanking him because you know you have believed that you received what you requested.

> And God's peace shall be yours, that tranquil state of a soul assured of its salvation through Christ. And not fearing nothing from God and being content with its earthly lot of whatever sort that is, that peace which transcend all understanding shall garrison and mount guard over your hearts and minds in Christ Jesus. For the rest brethren, whatever is true, whatever is worthy of reverence and is honorable and seemly, whatever is just, whatever is pure, whatever is lovely and lovable, whatever is kind and winsome and gracious, if there is any virtue and excellence, If there is anything worthy of praise, think on and weigh and take account of these things [fix your mind on them]. Practice what you have learned and received and heard and seen in me, and model your way of living on it, and the God of peace (of untroubled, undisturbed well-being) will be with you. (Philippians 4:7–9 AMP)

Now fix your mind on these things! None of this will work unless you do it. Keep on doing it until you get the victory. Then make it your lifestyle.

Serve God or Money

Man must look inside himself and change his mind for good. I had to look deep inside myself and decide if I really wanted life and health or death and the curse. When we prepare ourselves for the soul business, and that is to get people saved and converted, we must send sincere prayers to God and turn our prayers over to him. We must give in to him and honor the covenant we have with him. If there is any sin that remain in us and we still practice it, we must drop it like it is hot and put it far from us. Whatever benefits we gained from sin must be abandoned. We must do the utmost to get all our family members to Christ. Get all evil out of our homes, bodies, and wealth gotten by wickedness. Then we will be able to come into the presence of God with a clean hearts and hands and not be afraid. We will be able to come to him correct, direct, and erect.

We want to be steadfast in our prayers as we submit to God, and he will keep us safe. God did not make us to be idle but that we should do the things that he called us to do for his kingdom. If we are doing his will, we will be under his divine protection. So "when you lie down you will not be afraid, Yea, thou shalt lie down and thou sleep shall be sweet, for the Lord shall be thy confidence and shall keep thy foot from being taken."

Proverbs 11:7 says, "When the wicked man dieth, his expectation shall perish, and the hope of the unjust men perish." Their hope vanishes like the fog on your car windshield when the defrost is turned on. Many rich people mock God's people and live easy and good lives without God. They think they have everything, but they don't know. Revelation 2:9 (KJV) tells us, "I know thy works, and tribulation, and poverty, /(but thou art rich) and I know the blasphemy of them which say they are Jews, and are not, but are of the synagogue of Satan."

The rich despise the poor because it is the way of the world. People love us when we are on the top but despise us when we are at the bottom. We must remember that all souls belong to God. If we don't have the wisdom and the strength of God, we will become our own gods and become foolish, and that will make God lose the fruit that he should be getting from his creation. The only thing that can get rid of sin guilt is repentance. We must admit it, quit it, get back with it, and get in line with theWordofGod.

Our time and our walk here on earth is very limited and uncertain, and we must make every minute and step count. Our lives are on a day- to-day plan, and who knows if today will be their last? On top of that, our days are full of trouble; if it's not one thing going wrong, it's another. We are never satisfied because either it's too hot, too cold, or too rainy. We are always complaining about something. We must keep our faith moving forward not fearing and having hope in God as we walk in love. Our way is hiding in God, and as we walk with him, we must keep our faith and hope alive. We must ask God to help us understand his way for our lives. Job 14:7–14 explains how man is cut down like a tree; that makes the soul business so important. Verse 7 tells us, "For there is hope of a tree, if it be cut down, that it will spout again, and that the tender branch thereof will not cease." We die, and our spirits leave our bodies, which are hidden in a grave until the trumpet sounds.

We get used to the things of the world, but we can't take them with us. Our confidence should be in God and his plan for us after death. Being Christlike and fearing God should be our focus. We should not put our hopes in man because he is a puff of smoke and dust. Hopeless people who do not pray are fearless. We must pray so we don't give those who would like to harm us opportunity to succeed. Job said, "Who can bring a clean thing out of an unclean thing but he that is born again of the spirit who becomes clean." Those who love sin are miserable, and misery loves company.

Even some of the rich are miserable because the money they hustled, schemed, and sinned for is basically spent on other sins. They can't see their fall, and some see it coming and are scared to death. They are afraid because horrible sin brings horrible punishment. Most people I talk to have heard of God, but they would rather serve mammon, which is gain. They say it is easier to commit sin than to serve God.

We must keep our hope alive in Jesus Christ. We must have that earnest, intense, favorable, confident expectation in God. Those who are absent from the body are present with the Lord. We are always anticipating his coming as we focus on God and his Word. The end of our personal worlds is coming, and we do not know the day or hour.

The Glory of God

The glory of God refers to the supernatural existence outside the natural world and intervenes in it to do the miraculous. The glory of God has everything we need. The Israelites saw the glory of God in the pillar of cloud by day and a pillar of fire by night (Exodus 13:21).

I saw God's glory when I was hit by a car in 1999 and knocked eight feet up in the air and landed on the windshield. They lost my pulse twice on the way to the hospital, where I was in a coma for fifteen days. When I came out the coma, I was paralyzed. My c-4 and c-5 in my neck had me paralyzed. My left ankle and knee were broken along with my right femur and right wrist. My jaw was broken in two places, and my tongue was cut in half. The power of God blessed me to walk out of the nursing home as I displayed his glory. I came out of my paralysis and was able to stand up, look you in the eye, and tell you how good Jehovah had been to me. God gave me a new life in him.

In Habakkuk 3:4, God appeared in his glory; God came from Teman, and even the holy one from Mount Paran was a visible display of God's glory. The same glory was seen on Mount Sinai in Deuteronomy 33:3; it covered the heavens and the earth and was full of his praise. Ezekiel saw God in his glory and said that he was a fire from the loins up and from the loins down. The fire of God is his glory. The wind is his glory. His fullness is his glory. Sometimes, we see Christians on fire for God just after getting saved, and that is a good example of God's glory.

God's essence goes beyond the natural forces of this world, and his glory makes him who he is. Man was surrounded by God's glory and was like a fire round about him. That's why Adam and Eve could not see their nakedness. Exodus 24:17 says, "And the sight of the glory of the Lord was like devouring fire on top of the mount in the eyes of the children of Israel." The glory of the Lord was lost on Adam and Eve when they sinned but was restored when Jesus was resurrected.

Romans 6:4 says, "Therefore we are buried with him by baptism into death: that like as Christ was raised up from the dead by the glory of the Father, even so we also should walk in newness of life." Praising God is acknowledging his perfection and his doing good in our lives. What God does for us cannot be comprehended. We must own him and claim him on the housetops, not in the closet. L give him the praises of my lips. We should always be bragging on God and serving him with our whole hearts, bodies, and souls.

The Blame Game of Satan

Ever since Satan lied to himself wanting to be God, he has been playing the blame game. Satan blamed God in the garden of Eden telling his creation that God was holding out on them. Satan twisted God's Word and made Adam and Eve part of his disobedient family. The devil spits in our hands and tells us it's raining to keep us from seeing the truth, which is the only thing that makes us free. John 17:17 says, "Sanctify them through thy truth thy word is truth."

The enemy gives us a different perspective on God and his Word. The only thing Satan has left is his deception. He will tell us that the Word cannot help us through our situations and problems. If we are going to live free, we can't be listening to negative words, doubt, and the do-nothings. Rahab's people say, "Stop telling me your visions. Don't tell me the truth. Just make me feel good with some more painkillers. Stop telling me about God." Don't they know their souls are at stake? Deuteronomy 28:15 says, "All these curses will come upon you." Keep speaking God's Word if things look like they are changing or not. God's Word will open heaven for you to be blessed.

God doesn't care if we look at the answer book, the Bible, when questions and problems come our way. Going to church, hearing the preacher, and sharing with members are so important. Satan wants us to defeat ourselves, and we do that by speaking contrary to God's Word. The enemy does not want us to spread God's truth or his Word to make earth the Eden it is supposed to be. If we resist the enemy, he will flee from us (James 4:7), but he is masterful at keeping us from resisting him. We must stand against him in faith, which comes by hearing the Word of God.

The Bible says that a double-minded man is unstable in all his ways. Who can serve two masters? Satan is trying to keep us from giving God the glory. Look at the spirit working in people around you who want God's glory and you will get a good look at Satan. We must continue to spread the truth of God's Word. Satan has agents with different personalities who come against us including sickness, disease, persecution, and lack. We must stay plugged in to God. When our strength is depleted, God steps in and gives us his.

We can't let Satan's blame game keep us from saying what God says about our situations and conditions. Satan will try convincing us that there is no way out, but there is nothing too hard for God. The enemy wants us to get stuck in guilt, shame, and condemnation. When God is pleased with our management of his Spirit, he will give us his best. Proverbs 16:3 says, "Commit thy works unto the Lord, and thy thoughts shall be established." God will guide you even in times of misfortune and lift us when we are down.

> Fear thou not for I am with thee. Be not dismayed; for I am thy God; I will help thee; yea' I will uphold thee with the right hand of my righteousness. Behold, all they that were incensed against thee shall be ashamed and confounded: they shall be as nothing; and they that shall strive with thee shall perish. Thou shall seek them, and shall not find them, even them that contend with thee; they that war against thee shall be as nothing, and as a thing of naught. For I the Lord thy God will hold thy right hand, saying unto thee, Fear not; I will help thee. (Isaiah 41:10–13)

Be a Vessel of Honor

Children of God have the right to present their cases before God. Even sinners know whom to give their requests to. Our prayers will make it to the throne room of grace but theirs will not. We have the boldness to enter the holiest of holies because we have access to God and his Word. We can plead, ask, and argue because we are part of his family. God knew what was going on with that person before we showed up. God was glad to see that he had vessels that were encouraged enough for him to work through. God told Moses to go to Pharaoh and he would be like a God to him.

So are we when we are sent. "When God has tried me, I shall come forth as gold." God always has a destination for us. He wants us to be victorious in everything we do. We should inhale God's Word and speak it as we exhale.

Wealth

Wealth is the abundance of valuable material possessions or resources. We can also have a wealth of knowledge. Some people have hope in their money or education, but those will not be enough to save us from the grave. The wealthiest place on earth is the graveyard; that is where all the thoughts, dreams and ideas not acted upon lie. Some people don't share their talents; they take them to the grave with them. "Riches will not go on forever, nor do governments go on forever" (Proverbs 21:22 Everyday Bible).

Jesus Christ died, was buried, and rose victorious over the enemy and gave gifts to us according to our abilities. God placed a seed of greatness in all of us. When we are plugged in to God, he makes our thoughts wealthy. When they agree with his will, our plans will succeed.

Some are afraid to speak what God has laid on their hearts. They have a wealth of knowledge, but it is hidden in them, and they will never know what else God has for them. If they don't let it out and step up their worry, fret and fear will hold them back.

Don't bury your faith and the talents God gave you and wants you to show. If you step forward, a seed of greatness will bear much fruit. If you release the gift inside you, it will multiply. Whatever God has given you that you do best is your gift. It will bring forth much fruit in your and others' lives.

God asked Moses what was in his hand, and Moses told him a staff. God told him to stretch it out. Stop suppressing and compressing what you have because you think it is not enough. Instead, mix it with the Holy Spirit through prayer and put some corresponding action into it. I have stepped out of my box and started letting God do whatever he wants to do in me.

We should put all our trust in God. Some people put their trust only in money, but it says, "In God We Trust." They make money their god, but God is my money. "All the silver and gold is mine says the Lord." Yet they still get wealth the world's way. Their prayers will not be heard. They will do things in darkness and think no one sees, but God sees their sin. They put their confidence in money, but then they can't sleep because of the thought of losing it. They have sincere endeavors not knowing the dangers that are about to happen to them; their prosperity will be short lived, and they will end up miserable. Death, the king of terrors, will get them. We must trust God with our wealth, not trust in our wealth.

God's kingdom is a spiritual kingdom. The devil showed Jesus all the kingdoms of the world and told him that if he would only bow down and worship him, he would give them to him, but Jesus showed the enemy who really had all the silver and gold. Even today, Satan shows us the beginning but never shows us the end. The rich are so caught up in money that when death comes, they are afraid to go to the next world, where money has no power. "What if a man gains the whole world and lose his own soul?" "The wealth of the wicked is laid up for the just."

> He that by usury and unjust gain increases his substance, he will gather it for him that will pity the poor. He that turns away his ear from hearing the law, even his prayer shall be an abomination. Whoso causes the righteous to go astray in an evil way, he shall fall himself into his own pit: but the upright shall have good things in possession. The rich man is wise in his own conceit; but the poor that has understanding searches him out.
>
> He that covers his sins shall not prosper: but when the wicked rise, a man is hidden. Happy is the man that fears always: but he that hardens his heart shall fall into mischief. (Proverbs 28:8–11, 13–14 KJV)

Death comes in a hurry to carry the wicked away in a violent and dreadful way. When a man has peace with God, his death gets him to heaven, but the sinner will be a miserable person after death. His soul will be cursing God. It will be too late to choose life and peace after we die, but God's hand is still stretched out to us. We cannot run or hide from God's judgment. The poor must look at themselves closely; they might desire wealth, but that desire can ensnare them. Just as people did not understand Jesus's making the blind see and the lame walk, getting rich is a mystery to the poor; they lack restraint and prudence.

The rich delight in wealth and monopolies, but the poor need effective instruction on how to create and keep wealth. Daniel 8:23 speaks of dark sentences, Daniel 5:12 show us the need to understand hard sentences, and divine sentences are covered in Proverbs 16:10. The poor understood it not and it becomes a riddle to them. For those who need God's wisdom, pray the following prayer.

To Obtain and Maintain a Godly Character

> Lord, increase my faith and Father God I pray to you to receive wisdom and discipline, I ask you for the ability to understand words of insight. By your grace I am acquiring a discipline and prudent life, doing what is right just and fair. I thank you lord for giving me prudence, knowledge and discretion. As a wise person I listen and add to my learning, and as a discerning person I accept guidance {So that I may be able to steer my course rightly}. I thank you Father that I understand Proverbs, Parables, the saying and riddles of the wise in the mighty name of Jesus Christ. (*Prayers That Avail Much for Men*, Jermaine Copeland, page 12)

Crab Mentality

There are always those with a crab mentality who will try to hold you back from reaching the top; they will try to trip you up. This is when you must keep your focus and keep moving forward in the things of God. Don't be afraid of the power of the wealth of those who have it; just ask them how they came about it. Do not let your sins define your steps to a better life. Evil men have their hearts set on the things of the world, and they are not concerned about leaving it.

The world takes care of its own, and sometimes, evil men get rich and seemingly set the standard of wealth for others. Worldly people's portion is in this life, but we can have abundance in this life and hearts touched by love; we should be thankful and obediently do what is good with wealth. We will thus be fruitful, and it will abound to our account. Some set their hearts on the best things; they trust in their wealth, and they depend on it as their portion, and it becomes their happiness. Their gold is their hope. Job 31:24 reads, "If I have made gold my hope, and have said to the fine gold; Thou art my confidence." Then wealth becomes their god. The saints say that God is their money, but the world says money is its god.

It is very difficult to give salvation to the rich. We worry about the crabs, but sometimes, our own trust in money can do us in. "How hard it is for those that have riches to enter the kingdom of God" (Mark 10:24). "For he brought nothing into this world, and certainly can carry nothing out" (Timothy 6:7). "For the Love of money is the root of all evil: which while some coveted after, they have erred from the faith, and pierced themselves through with many sorrows" (1 Timothy 6:10). We should tell the rich not to trust in riches but in the living God who gives us richly all things to enjoy. The rich think that their houses will last forever, and they are pleased with that thought. Remind them not to think that tomorrow is promised and lay up treasures for many years (Luke 12:19–20).

Luke 12:16–20 says, "The ground of a certain rich man brought forth plentifully." He had a lot of ground. That was what was in his heart. He did not think of the good that he could do with it but worried about his money. Some people cannot sleep thinking about their wealth. This rich man was a careful manager of his wealth. He said, "I will pull down my barns and build greater and there bestow all my fruits and my goods." God lends us money and things so that we can be stewards of them. That man wanted to hoard what he had and not share with the poor, strangers, and widows. He had an exaggerated opinion of his importance. He never let his thoughts become agreeable to God's will so that his plans would be established and succeed. He had a me, myself, and I attitude. He said, "I will say to my soul, Soul thou hast much goods laid up for many years,

now take thine ease, eat drink, and be merry" (v. 19). He wanted to satisfy the flesh not thinking of others and his own soul.

God said to him, "Thou fool, this night Thy soul shall be required of thee then who's shall those things be, which thou hast provided? For a man's life consist not in the abundance of things which he possessed." Our happiness does not depend on wealth. The things of the world will not satisfy our souls at death. Verse 21 states, "So is he that latest up treasures for himself and is not rich toward God. He lay up treasure for this world and laid none toward the world where he was destined to go to." This put the man in opposition to God. I know people who are shooting to become wealthy and don't have time for God and his commands. They should obey God and accept his will for their lives. Jesus wants us to deny self and follow him. He counted those things his treasures, not money.

The love of money and the world is a disease that runs through our blood until it meets with God's grace. Yes, money helps us get what we need, but everlasting life is more valuable than all the gold and silver on earth. God dropped manna from the sky, but it lasted for only a time just as money does.

Christ did what all the riches of the world could not do, what no one else could do. Whoever loves his or her father, mother, sister, or brother more than him is not worthy of him. Jesus said, "Take no thought for your life what ye shall eat or what ye shall put on." We should "Seek Him first, and his righteousness, and his way of doing and being right and all these other things shall be added unto you."

Disciples Should Observe the Miners

The wealth of this world is hidden in the earth, and miners dig for it. Gold can adorn us, but God is concerned about our inner selves. Man came from dust; God breathed life into him, and he became a living soul. Our souls are more valuable than all gold and silver. When God made us, he put the earth under our feet and the heavens above. The wisdom of God kept precious metals out of our sight so we could walk on them and not praise them.

Adam and Eve were rich in God above, not in the gold and silver beneath their feet, but when they sinned, they lost their riches in God and became spiritually broke. Instead of looking up, they looked down and praised things on the earth. Their heads were hanging because of guilt, shame, and condemnation. They were looking for their next meal. A couple who once had everything were locked out of paradise.

Man started finding things in the earth to make himself useful. Man found everything to do in and on the earth except walk with God. Have you noticed people who are always looking down instead of looking up to God? This is where witnessing and prayer can get them to look to their creator for their needs. We must point them in the right direction, to the creator, and lead them to Christ.

In Genesis 4:2, Cain was looking for self-worth. He wanted what his brother had and could not understand that God would have done the same for him; but the spirit of jealousy came upon him. Men turned their backs on God for what they found under the earth, which made their eyes shine and their toes tingle. They started to worship things that God created, not their creator.

Man works hard to gain precious metals when what he should do is dig into God's Word until he finds the treasure in him, the true buried treasure. The Holy Spirit is your treasure. I dig into God's Word because it helps me through every situation; God guides me to all truth, my real treasure. I will not leave any stone in the Word of God unturned until his perfect plan for my life manifests itself and I receive what he has for me. God perfects whatever concerns me.

Adam and Eve were supposed to multiply and spread Eden across the earth. When lust for silver and gold popped up, prostitution came along. Satan used God's plan for mankind to be fruitful and multiply to make a living off it by pimping and prostitution, one of his tricks. Prior to that, there was no lusting after the flesh, and precious metals in the garden of Eden were in the ground they walked on.

When they were kicked out of the perfect garden, Adam and Eve did not know how to make it in the world. Humankind went through a lot of hurt and pain, but even death did not deter people from lusting after wealth and forgetting about God. People are dying today because they do not know what true wealth is. Few men and women really know the value of life. If God's people would search for the true riches the way miners do, they would be in a wealthy place in God. Anything that has worth is not easily obtained. Precious metals have to be mined, gold and silver can be stolen, and people can be killed for their money. Riches come at a cost.

God was trying to get the Israelites to a wealthy place, but all they did was murmur and complain. Just as miners find different ways to uncover precious metals, we Christians should find different ways to find God and get closer to him. We can read the Bible, pray, praise him, and buy tapes. We can watch different Christian programs because faith comes by hearing the Word of God. One word from God can change our lives. Some believers want to be spoon-fed the Word only once a week. They won't be able to withstand their hurts and pains. We should not forsake getting together with our fellow Christians and assisting each other when someone falls into sin. We have to say, "Who's on the Lord's side? Come over here!" The miners' path is not easy; they go where no man has gone before. Miners put their lives on the line for precious metals. Reading about Solomon will give you some knowledge about God and his love for those who seek him with all their mind, heart, and soul. Strong men of God are successful in the things of God, and they got there working hard like miners. People want the wealth pastors have but don't want to put their lives on the line for God. These men and women bring all things that are hidden to the light just as God brought the world out of darkness into light. People of God are not that light, but they testify about it. They remind me of myself. I am not wealthy, but I bet they are somewhere now bragging on God. You get rewards for bragging on Jehovah God.

We Christians should courageously, diligently, and persistently seek the wealth that never perishes, the true riches that are in God. We should come out of our laziness and not give up when hard times and persecution come our way. We should labor for true riches—knowing God and ourselves. We don't know the price of mercy and grace that God is willing to give us, and we don't have to go through the same pain the miners go through. We can't put a price on wisdom. All we must do is make a daily sacrifice and commune with God, who will supply all our needs.

Acts 8:9 (KJV) reads, "But there was a certain man, called Simon, which before time in the same city used sorcery, and bewitched the people of Samaria, giving out that himself was some great one." President Donald Trump, who has great wealth, is becoming some great one. The gift of the Holy Spirit cannot be bought; gold will make you appear rich, but wisdom is for the soul and eternity. The fear of the Lord is the beginning of wisdom. We should ask, "Where can we find wisdom?" not "Where's the money?" The only true wisdom is from God. If we don't know God's purpose and will for our lives, we can discover it in his Word. Those who are born again have access to the wisdom of God. Those who walk as Jesus walked have God's wisdom. Job 28:133 (KJV) reads, "Man knoweth not the price thereof; neither is it found in the land of the living." You will find true wisdom only by digging into God's Word.

Meditate on God's Word day and night and you will find wisdom. God has wisdom he reveals to us. We cannot know God's secret will for our lives. Knowing why God does what he does is the knowledge of God. Job 28:21 (KJV) reads, "Seeing it [wisdom] is hiding from the eyes of all the living and kept close from the fowls of the air." Before you get to smart and want to be your own god and let Satan give you his pride, say this prayer with me from *The Prayers that Avail Much for Men* by Jermaine Copeland, "Godly Wisdom in the Affairs of Life," page 4.

Prayer: Godly Wisdom in the Affairs of Life (by Jermaine Copeland)

> Father, you said if anyone lacks wisdom let him ask of you, who giveth to all men liberally, and upbraided not; and it shall be given him. Therefore, I ask in faith nothing wavering, to be filled with the knowledge of your will in all wisdom and spiritual understanding. Today I incline mine ear unto wisdom and apply my heart to understanding so that I might receive that which has been freely given to me.
>
> In the name of Jesus, I receive skill and Godly wisdom and instruction. I discern and comprehend the words of understanding and insight. I receive instructions in wise dealing and the discipline of wise thoughtfulness, righteousness, justice and integrity, prudence, knowledge, discretion and discernment are given to me. I increase in knowledge. As a person of understanding, I acquire skill and attain to sound counsels (so that I may be able to steer my course rightly).
>
> Wisdom will keep, defend and protect me, I love her, and she guards me. I prize Wisdom highly and exalt her, she will bring me to honor because I embrace her. She gives to my head a wrath of gracefulness; a crown of beauty and glory will she deliver to me. Length of days is in her right hand, and In her left hand are riches and

honor. Jesus has made unto me wisdom, and in Him are all the treasures of (divine) wisdom {of comprehensive insight into the ways and purposes of God} and {all the riches of spiritual knowledge and enlightenment are stored up and lie hidden. God has hidden away sound and godly wisdom and stored it up for me, for I am the righteousness of God in Christ Jesus.

Therefore, I will walk in the path of uprightness. When I walk, my steps shall not be hampered-my path will be clear and open: and when I run, I shall not stumble, I take fast hold of instructions, and do not let her go, I guard her for she is my life. I let my eyes look right on {with a fixed purpose} and my gaze is straight before me. I consider well the path of my feet, and I let all my ways be established and ordered aright.

Father in the name of Jesus, I look carefully to how I walk! I live purposely and worthily and accurately, not as unwise and witless, but as a wise, sensible intelligent person, making the very most of my time –buying up every opportunity Amen.

We must use our intellects to dig up the wisdom God has for us.

Public Nuisance

The world is full of poor people who were driven from among men or walked away from their homes. When we fail to live up to a standard of conduct, we naturally feel guilty, ashamed, and condemned. Some beg for alms to get by daily. In 1 Kings 7:3 (Everyday Bible), we read, "Why do we sit here until we die? So, they got up and went." Some impoverished people can't find jobs, and others have limiting physical conditions or drug habits or are just plain lazy. Many beggars were driven into the woods because of their persistent begging. Many have alcohol problems. A lot have mental problems and cannot manage their lives. There are some who let their demons get the best of them.

Paupers are very poor people who rely on charity and live in public housing. If they are not encouraged to work, some will not. There are many reasons people become poor, but frequently, it's because they lived by the wrong standards. Some street people are stuck in guilt and will not get up and do anything for themselves. Jesus gave a way out of sin to all who ask for it. If you can be productive, you can fit in with the well-to-do crowd. Don't get me wrong; some well-dressed bums are trying to fit in.

Beggars ask for your spare change or something to eat and ask for help with their bills. They need help, but their conduct interferes with the legal rights of others by causing damage, annoyance, and inconvenience. Satan and society use false guilt to manipulate people. That is irritating and troublesome harassment that vexes the spirits of those they confront. I knew a lot of people who ignored their consciences and lied, cheated, and stole feeling like they were doing the right thing to survive. Their consciences had become hardened (1 Timothy 4:1–20). We are living in very uncertain times, and we all have reasons to be concerned but not to worry. God's people's lives are built on a solid rock, Jesus, and all other grounds are quicksand.

We must pray for kings and all who are in authority. The Bible has a few beggars in it, but they were lame. The Bible states, "If a man doesn't work, he doesn't eat." True believers must pray for those in authority that God will give them his judgment and righteousness. Isaiah 11:4 says, "But with righteousness shall he Judge the poor, and reprove with equity for the meek of the earth: and he shall smite the earth with the rod of his mouth, and with the breath of his lips shall he slay the wicked." Christ showed us how to be fair and impartial. God has a special peace, the glory of his kingdom, which brings men to Christ Jesus. The peace of God is spread from one to another. This happens when hearts meet. People's hearts meet at Christmas, but that should happen every day. The peace of God removes all bad thoughts because Jesus came to give us peace. Our government has the responsibility to care for and protect those in need. God will save the poor who are oppressed, and the oppressors will receive his judgment. Bad choices and Satan are behind all the oppression that goes on in our lives, but God will break the power of Satan's pride and destroy his works. The blood of the saints is very precious to God; not a drop should be shed by deception and violence in our society. All believers are protected under the blood of Jesus. Christ is not a buster; he is a king who calls his angels and saints to run errands for him.

Sometimes, we resist our callings as Jonah did. Sometimes, many saints magnify Christ in their living as David did and if necessary in dying also. We must have the law written in our hearts because God wants us to walk in love wherever he puts us. He does this so we will produce abundant peace and beat swords into plowshares. God will have a kingdom of peace and love so that all men will fear God. The gospel of Christ is almost all over the earth. Don't think that those who are not saved are not fearing the Second Coming of Christ just as when the Israelites pitched their camp in the plains of Moab on the other side of the Jordan (Numbers 22). The world sees God's people the same way, but we want to come out together to put the fear of God in their hearts.

All the saints need to do is appear. "And Moab was sore afraid of the people, because they were many: and Moab was distressed because of the children of Israel." Their hearts needs to be melted and their wrong spirits taken out of them (Deuteronomy 32:16–17). They have provoked God to jealousy by worshipping strange gods. Verse 18 says, "Of a Rock that begat thee thou art unmindful, and hast forgotten God that formed thee."

Our nation is void of counsel and understanding because people do not consider their end. In verse 30, God said, "How should one chase a thousand and two put ten thousand to flight, except their Rock had sold them and the Lord had shut them up." In verses 32–33, we read, "For their vine is the vine of Sodom, and of the fields of Gomorrah, their grapes are the grapes of gall their clusters are bitter. Their wine is the poison of dragons, and the cruel venom of apps." God said in verses 37–40,

> And he shall say, where are their gods, their rock in whom they trusted, Which did eat the fat of their sacrifices, and drink the wine of their drink offering? Let them rise up and help you and be your protection. See now that I even I am he, and there is no God with me, I kill and I make alive; wound, and I make alive, I wound, and I heal, neither is there any that can deliver out of my hand. For I lift up my hand to heaven, and say, I live forever. (Deuteronomy 32:16–18, 30, 32–33, 37–40 KJV)

The Word of God will be written in their hearts, and they will focus on God.

Penitent

To be penitent is to be truly sorry for our sin and be willing to atone for them by rejoicing in our return to God and leaving the world behind. When we repent, we ask God to forgive us for not obeying him and for trying to be our own gods. I ask God to help me to see the light of what he has planned for my life and the fruit he has for me. Help me, Father, to see myself through your eyes.

Fruition means coming to fulfillment. All God is trying to do is work in us; we should be working with him having one harmonious mind and intention—to keep man's soul from going to hell and to bless him in our journey on earth. The soul is the most important part of a human being. Anything that is trying to condemn your soul is a great evil. Our eyes and ears could be our enemies because they are gateways to our hearts. We must guard our eyes and hearts from evil so we do not miss out on our God-ordained destinies. God sees how we walk, where we are walking, whom we are walking with, and the company we keep to make sure we don't get off course. He sees our wrong steps when we are supposed to be doing his will.

Our eyes can lead us to hell unless they are fixed on the Word of God. We shouldn't let our hearts hang out with our eyes unless our eyes are fixed on the Word of God and his plan for our lives. We must keep our eyes from coveting anything. A Temptations song is titled, "Don't Let the Jones Get you Down." People get in all sorts of financial trouble trying to keep up with the Joneses. Covetousness is a sin. In 1 John 2:16 (KJV), we learn, "For all that is in the world, the lust of the flesh, and the lust of the eyes, and the pride of life is not of the Father but is of the world." Covertness is the lust of the eyes, and we need to keep our mouths, eyes, and hearts from sin. Lust and covertness can burn our souls.

Christians who find themselves lusting after something will spend their energy trying to get rid of that lust and overcome temptation. We must take care of our souls before we can help others with theirs. We should be crucified with Christ. The lust of the flesh is called luxury, things used for pleasure or things that are hard to obtain—a big house or expensive car—while drowning in gold jewelry. The lust of the eyes is called covetousness. The pride of life is called an excessive desire for honor, power, or wealth. They must all be put away. Friendship with the world is anenemyofGod.

If we don't repent for our sins, we will face eternal damnation and punishment, the state the wicked will fall into.

Covertness

People can stop seeking the praise of God and start seeking the praise of others and the power the world has to offer. We must teach them the Word of God. Satan has offered this generation all the kingdoms of the world, and they have fallen for it and become violent and uncontrolled animals. They like to display terror, but they will run into the king of terrors—death—if they don't get saved. They use religion as a cloak for their personal ambitions.

Good people are caught up in hypocritical schemes. Sometimes when we pray, we are not sorry for our sin and we cry out to God. We become friends of the world when we are caught up in pleasures, prosperity, and fleshly things rather than God's mercy and grace. This happens when we do not seek God first. We have God on the back burner when trouble comes. We should try to get him involved in our matters and afflictions for all answers in life.

We hear people asking, Where's the money? Where's a good job? Where's a good place to eat or have fun? Where is Big Booty Sue or Hanging John? Who is asking, Where is my God? God provides for our peace of mind and gives us happiness. He teaches and cultivates us when trouble comes our way, and he saves us from distress. God's grace helps work deliverance for those who don't serve him. They expect his benefits and have the capability of asking God, but they leave him out of their affairs.

Sometimes, God does not work deliverance because of the pride or the iniquity in the hearts of those who are being their own gods. God will not hear their prayers because of the sin in their hearts. Isaiah 1:15–16 (KJV) says, "And when ye spread forth your hands, I will hide my eyes from you: yea, when ye make many prayers, I will not hear: your hands are full of blood." If you are not on the Lord's side, you will be left in your afflictions. It will not be because God can't help you; it will be because you haven't humbled yourself enough.

"For let not that man think that he shall receive any thing of the Lord" (James 1:7 KJV). God allows affliction on the righteous for their own good. God allowed Joseph to be in jail, but he covered him all the way through that affliction. Joseph was faithful and never blamed God, and he had the favor of God. This was part of his growth and development. His soul was being cultivated. God wants us to mirror ourselves on his Word so we will reflect him. It helps us see our sin so we will be able to hear his instructions. God wants us to resemble Jesus as we wear the seal of the New Testament, and that was by his blood.

God gives us his grace and mercy to carry us through though we don't deserve it. Every day, God gives us another opportunity to get it right. This was so the affliction will accomplish what it was sent to do. When we are delivered, we should confess, "It shall not arise a second time." I was afflicted by being paralyzed, and I did not feel comforted until I surrendered to God. I became one with him, and he did all the work and fought all my battles. I started doing the promises faithfully and received God's glory for everything good that came into my life. I went to college, and God blessed me with a new car and a three-bedroom house. God blessed me inside and out by giving me a new focus on life. He made me an encourager of the brethren. I passed out tracts and witnessed everywhere I went giving God all the glory, honor, and praise. I bragged on him everywhere I went. God supplied me with the Holy Spirit to magnify what was already in me to build others up.

The joy of the Lord was my strength, and the peace of Christ ruled my heart. I am thankful for his grace and the power of the Holy Spirit. I am glad my affliction worked in me, and I never once blamed or cursed God because of the choices I had made. When I was in the world, I chose death instead of life. I chose the curse instead of the blessing. I am so glad that I did not get God's judgment. I was saved, and I was playing the role of a coward because I was one of God's kingdom's secret enemies. I was a coward running from God like Adam and Eve did ducking and hiding while covering up their sins. My heart was hardened, but I did not know that. I was being hardheaded, rebellious, and disobedient. I am so glad God did not let Satan take me out in my sin. I am so glad God changed my opinion of myself and made me face life head-on. Sin was a disease in my life, and I spread it everywhere I went. I thank God for the remedy—repentance—and the blood of Jesus Christ.

Many people have never heard about God or don't want to believe he exists. I know prostitutes and thieves who spread the epidemic of lust and fornication like wildfire. Getting saved stops a multitude of sins. Drug dealers run around all day long with a bag of curses. God's Word says, "The fool has said in his heart that there is no God." They believe there is no creator though the Bible tells them, "And God breathed the breath of life into man and man became a living soul." All they have to do is inhale and exhale. It will be too late after death. They are fools for being far from God. Those without the knowledge of God become beasts who choose wrong paths.

"They have become putrid, morally corrupt, decayed, decomposed, and rotten." They don't do themselves or God any good. They find themselves fighting against the answer—God. Some people do good works but deny God. But they can have crises, Damascus road experiences, and pray that God will change them. In Genesis 1:3, God looked at what he made and considered it very good. But in Genesis 6:5, we read, "And God saw that the wickedness of man was great in the earth and that every imagination of the thoughts of his heart was only evil continually."

God is concerned about the wickedness and the danger his children are in. The unsaved take pleasure in sin. They love to feast on God's people because of their giving spirits. They have the knowledge of the world but don't know all the terror that the devil can bring them. Some people worship Satan by drinking blood as a sacrifice to do evil deeds. On the other hand, Jesus's shed blood paid for our sins. Bread symbolizes Jesus's broken body, and wine symbolizes his shed blood. He focused on dying and suffering, and he was not moved from being able to say, "It is finished." Jesus was on an errand to keep his Word that he had spoken through the prophets and the disciples. Jesus had a fixed purpose and a determined mission. When we are on our missions for God, we should not waver, hesitate, or doubt but do them cheerfully.

We should use Jesus as our example and use the glory of our tongues to give God the glory in what we do. "I have set the Lord always before me." "Seeking God's kingdom, His righteousness and His way of doing and being right and all these other things will be added unto me." We should be confident of God's presence with us. He is a very present help in trouble and nigh at hand in time of our every need. Hebrews 10:22 (KJV) says, "Let us draw near with a true heart in full, assurance of faith, having our hearts sprinkled from an evil conscience, and our bodies washed, washed with pure water."

"Looking unto Jesus the author and finisher of our faith, who for the joy that was set before him endured the cross, despising the shame, and is set down at the right hand of the throne of God" (Hebrews 12:2). We should rest in Jesus.

> And in that day there shall be a root of Jesse, which shall stand for an ensign of the people; to it shall the Gentiles seek: and His rest shall be glorious. Now is the judgment of this world: now shall the prince of this world be cast out. And I, if I be lifted up from the earth, will draw all men unto me. (John 12:31–32)

Jesus was brought from under the powers of death by being resurrected. I thank you, Father God, for you will guide me through the valley of the shadows of death. We should always let our consciences watch over our souls.

Dangers of Marijuana

Our society has changed so much that we can hardly recognize it. Marijuana, legal or illegal, is a danger to health. Men's and women's social roles have changed. We face national and international security issues from social media. We have evolving gender definitions, and we see government and media trying to convince us that right is wrong and wrong is right. We are moving toward destruction through abominations and bad choices for the economy.

These choices are for money and not for the soul. We all have rights and a choice. God reads us our rights in his Word, but America chooses to give up those rights. God penned his Word through man.

"His Word is settled in heaven." It "is the same yesterday, today and forever." Now we have gay Bibles and women's Bibles that show a division in God's kingdom, but God is no respecter of persons. Marijuana showed up strong during the social revolution in the 1960s when free love was introduced to the Western world. This was the hippie movement that seems closely related to the savage generation of today's youth that says anything goes.

Marijuana is being used for medical purposes, and it is now legal in some states. Most of this generation has rejected God's moral values and have turned to hallucinogenic drugs. Marijuana has become America's new cash crop. America has said that if it doesn't make money, it doesn't make sense. Gay marriage was a good investment for the United States. You can marry anybody or anything because it added to the economy and this is the land of the free. America is saying, "If you like it, we love it for the money." America is desperate and greedy. Now we have marijuana growers in competition with organized crime. Since we can't beat them, might as well join them. America says give me some of that money. They are still trying to find a way they can make their hands happy by receiving some of that money. Legalizing marijuana is a good way to receive votes.

We should honor and respect God's Word, which tells us to care for our bodies because they are God's temples. In 1 Corinthians 6:19 (LB), we read, "Haven't you yet learned that your body is the home of the Holy Spirit God gave you, and that he lives within you." The Holy Spirit lives in Christians; our bodies are not our own. We are possessed by and for God. We were purchased by Jesus's blood. Our bodies were made by and for God. Our lives are candles that burn out. We must apply ourselves to God. Man is flesh and spirit. Heaven and earth were put together in him so he could be of both worlds. God said in Genesis 1:26–27 (LB), "Let us make man someone like ourselves, to be the master of all life upon the earth and in the skies and in the seas. So God made man like his Maker … Like God did God make man … Man, and Maid did he make them." There is still a distance between God and man. Jesus, who has the same nature as Jehovah our God does, was clothed with a body like ours, and shortly, we will be clothed in glory like his.

People think marijuana has no ill effects. Organized crime makes money on illegal sales, and the government is asking, "Where mine?" The average person still asks, "What can be wrong with legalizing a harmless substance and denying criminals a market?" There is opposition not just from ultraconservatives or the religious movement but by a host of medical researchers.

The pro-marijuana lobby has done little research because their eyes and hearts are on that mean green. Medical research has found out that marijuana is a hallucinogen. Those who use it are unmotivated to work and to protect our country. This is the root of the "I can do whatever I want to do" problem. We don't need soldiers nodding off at their posts.

Long-term marijuana use can lead to addiction, and it can harm brains that are still developing and make younger people become hardheaded, rebellious, and disobedient at home and at school. "When there is no limit to the user, they can develop Brain Impairments-Reduced Memory- Attention Span and Reasoning," says Stuart Wachowicz. "Psychosis can develop when the family has a history of mental illness. This substance damages maturing brains and effects your decision making causing a thinning of the developing brains cortex." (*Tomorrow's World*, November– December 2017, "Marijuana: What They are Not Telling You").

We must stand against any type of drugs being legalized; we should be most concerned about the youth of this country because they are the future. Who wants to be slapping and shaking our coworkers on the job? We want our youth to have clear heads. How would you feel if someone had to watch over you full of drugs?

Health Canada's website informs us,

> There is a decline in physical coordination and reaction time. Marijuana can also affect an unborn child if the mother use during pregnancy. The toxins from marijuana are carried through the mother's blood to her fetus. It also goes to the breast milk after pregnancy. There are long term effects on the child as though they have been using for years.

There are many people who have gone on a mission and ended up dead or in jail. They are still wondering, *How did I get here?*

> Tetrahydrocannabinol or THC is still a threat to smoking pot. It is to 5 times to be a threat than cigarettes because of the level of Carbon monoxide This brings a loss of Cilla in the lungs. Causing emphysema. These are some of the same people who worry about cigarettes but are care less about marijuana. When marijuana is much more damaging to the lung. It has also been found that marijuana use could be associated with vascular conditions with an increased risk of heart attack and stroke that are not clear yet.

People who have an irregular heartbeat, or arrhythmia because it activates the sympathetic nervous system. This is when your blood pressure increases and heart rate increase. When the bloods ability to carry oxygen from the lungs to the rest of body is reduced. This put a strain on the heart and reduce the ability to handle increased demands. (Legalized Marijuana and Your Heart).

There are facts about the dangers of marijuana to human health and well-being whether it's legal or not. There is no reason to experiment on Americans. This is step in brainwashing, and the media and passing laws are the other two steps.

Prayer

Prayer is a psalm we pray to God. There is a time of praise after prayer knowing our prayers will be heard by God. This is the time for prayer, and we need it now more than ever. It is a great comfort when trouble comes to know we are already in communion with God. Praying in faith encourages us to expect God to consider our prayers. We know that God hears us while we are speaking. Every word we speak is a continual prayer whether it be a blessing or curse. "Life and death are in the power of the tongue." The spirit of man is a candle of the Lord. God searches man at night like he searched David at night as he had many opportunities to kill Saul. God searches our hearts and spirits all the time. His people had many enemies, but he delivered them from them all. These enemies were rebelling against God, but he used them like a whip on his own saints to keep them in line. God knows how to manage their actions against his saints. He can make the enemy not draw sword against his saints.

Cities all over the United States have been mentally kidnapped from evil by the removal of statues that reminded its citizens of the oppression of slavery. It will take America even longer to wake up from marijuana once it is totally submitted to it. Oppression and slavery are from Satan. God told Israel to tear down the idols, altars, and images. Jeremiah 50:39 tells us, "A drought is upon her waters and they shall be dried up: they are mad upon their idols. Declare ye among the nations and; publish and conceal not: say Babylon is broken in pieces; her idols are confounded; her images are broken in pieces." Jeremiah 50:2 says, "The Molten image is falsehood, there is no breath in them, they are vanity, the works of errors: in the time of their visitation they shall perish."

Prayer for the Protection and Deliverance of Our City and Nation

Father, in the name of Jesus Christ, we have received your power because the Holy Spirit has come upon us. We are your witnesses to the ends of the earth. We fearlessly draw near to the throne of grace to receive your mercy and well-timed help. Thank you for sending forth your commandments to the earth.

Your Word continues to spread all over the world, Father God. We ask for your peace to come to the world. We pray to you, Father God, for the welfare of our nation and the world. We will not let false prophets and diviners deceive us. Destroy their schemes, O Lord, and confuse their tongues for we have seen violence and strife.

Holy Spirit, open the eyes of our people so they turn from darkness to light and from the power of Satan to you, Jehovah God, so that they may receive forgiveness. Release them from their sins, and purify them in the name of Jesus Christ. We pray for salvation for those who are following the fashion of this world and are under the sway of the prince of the power of the air and the gods of this world that blind the unbelievers' minds to your truth.

We command you, Satan to leave in the mighty name of Jesus Christ. Thank you, Father, for the protection of your angels. In the mighty name of Jesus Christ, we stand victorious over the principalities, powers, rulers of darkness of this world, and spiritual wickedness everywhere. We ask the Holy Spirit to convince the people to seek right standing with God.

Father, you said in your Word, "For I know the thoughts that I think toward you, saith the Lord, thoughts of peace, and not of evil to give you an expected final outcome." Because of your favor, the United States of America is exalted. Father God, we believe we receive everything we pray for in the mighty name of Jesus Christ, amen. So be it unto us.

Deliverance

The greater the danger God delivers us from, the greater the mercy of that deliverance. God is always ready to bring his people back to him. Once we become honest and sincere about a situation or condition, deliverance can do its work and we can come out of our dark despair and into the knowledge of God. The Bible says, "Whosoever shall call on the name of the Lord shall be saved. And their soul abhors all manner of meat then they cry unto the Lord in their trouble and He saves them out of their distresses."

God has an invisible glory that he brings us out with. He is always keeping us from danger with his secret designs. When we come out, we know that it was nobody but God. He delivers his people out of their troubles and sustains them in their troubles to give them some breathing room. God is delighted in his children not because they are so nice but for his own grace and goodwill. Hebrews 5:7–10 states,

> Who in the days of his flesh, when he had offered up prayers and supplications with strong crying and tears unto him that was able to save him from death and was heard in that he feared. Though he were a Son, yet learned he obedience by the things which he suffered; And being made perfect, he became the author of eternal salvation unto all them that obey him. Called of God a high priest after the order of Melchiedec.

Those who are delivered and experience the love of God show their appreciation by praising him. Psalm 18 tells what David showed

God when God delivered him from his enemies. David said to God, "I will love thee, O Lord, my strength." David described the different ways God delivered him in verses 7–17, and he ended the psalm by giving God honor because God showed mercy on his anointed and all his seed.

When God delivers you, the evidence is clearly seen in you. The evidence before men shows how God acquitted you and brought you out of danger. The deliverance will show, and people will know you have been set free. God rewards us according to our righteousness.

Some people think that evil people can't make it out of their troubles, but God wants all men to be saved and come to repentance. We all stumble and fall, but if we repent and come to Jehovah, he will forgive us. God is merciful, and those who show mercy will find mercy with him. Matthew 5:7 tells us, "Blessed are the merciful for they shall obtain mercy." God had mercy on me so many times. He helped me through my danger and protected me from my enemies. God gave us specific gifts and talents for us to use in his kingdom. These will be the things we will take comfort in. I love music, and I can't count how many times a song came on the radio that told me to move or get up just in time. I remember a time when I was hanging out in the wrong neighborhood around people I didn't know. Everybody was trying to figure out who I was because I was confident, and they wanted to rob me and shut me up. Everybody was talking, and some were whispering. The Bible says that a whisperer separates the best of friends. When people whisper around me, I look for the door.

One time when some people were about to rob me, one of my favorite records came on: "Got to get up, got to get up, get on down." I heard that in my spirit because I felt uneasy in my stomach. When I got outside, someone told me that those people had been planning on robbing me. I told him about the song that had prompted me to get up and get on down. We laughed about that as we walked off in safety.

I thank God for his Holy Spirit, who gave me a love for music. "God will perfect that which concerns you." God will keep your feet from falling. One of my church member's sons hung out with a bad crowd. One night, they decided to play Russian roulette. My church member's son said they told him to try it first, and when he pulled the trigger, the gun did not go off. Then it was the next guy's turn. He pulled the trigger and killed himself. That was not all the young man went through. He was playing in a park one time when gunfire broke out, and a bullet grazed his arm. That incident delivered him from his friends, and he came to God. He was so on fire for the Lord that he would run through a troop and leap over a wall for the Lord. He had been given the shield of salvation because his mother prayed Psalm 91 over her kids even when they grew up and left the house. He had been delivered from those evil spirits that aimed to destroy him. Now, he praises, magnifies, blesses, exalts, and honors God. The Word of God has tried him and has not failed him. He believes God has subdued his enemies.

When I delighted myself in the Lord, he gave me a song that the angels cannot sing. God put a hedge around us, and we cannot exceed those boundaries.

The Word Written in Our Hearts

The Word of God should be in our hearts and on our lips. God's precepts are rules prescribing a course of action or conduct. His promises are declarations about what God will or will not do. They give us an indication of future success and favor because "God is not a man that He should lie neither the son of man that He has to repent." God's Word should be accepted without question.

To kill Goliath, David chose a smooth stone with no blemishes—Jesus. David knew that God was with him when he slew the lion and the bear. His experiences let him feel the presence of God. Meditate on God's Word and his promises and commune with him daily until you feel his presence. Run at your giants— problems, sickness, bad situations—with your smooth stone of the Word because God is bigger than any problem. The gospel is a proclamation of redemption preached by Jesus and the apostles. The Word of God brings us back to ourselves and to him so he can use us as his vessels. God's law in his Word gives us joy and peace and restores our souls and minds. Reading God's Word enlightens our spirits or inner man and helps it grow. Reading the Word of God gives us a mirror to help us see our sin sickness. The fear of the Lord is the beginning of wisdom, and the wisdom of God will help cleanse our way. Sin makes our lives miserable, but the Word cleans us up when we receive and use the precepts and promises of God by faith.

The Word of God is sweetness for the soul and health for the bones. The pleasures we receive from our senses are deceitful and only temporary fixes that we will continue to crave. God's Word makes us solid as a rock and strong enough to do his will. It helps us gain wealth, property, value, and a sense of importance. It makes real in our lives the things that we could not do on our own. We don't have to worry about taking an overdose of the Word. It tells us what we should be doing in God's kingdom and how to avoid danger. The Word is like warning signs on the roads of life; it gives us instruction on how to get out of our bondage. When we walk in obedience to God's Word, we are rewarded.

Psalm 103 shows us some of the benefits we will receive: "Who forgives all thine iniquities; who heals all thy diseases … Who redeems thy life from destruction; who crowns thee with loving kindness and tender mercies … Who satisfy thy mouth with good things; so that thy youth is renewed like the eagles." Yes, we get a reward for our obedience if we are in the will of God.

Our services to God are what we say and believe in our hearts. This is how we show our affection for God. When others desire to pray for us, they must not be turned down so their prayers will agree with ours. There is power in agreement. People will hate us because God has set us apart for himself. They also hated Jesus, the light of the world. John 15:23–25 says,

> He that hated me hated my Father also. If I had not done among them the works which none other man did, they had not sin, but now have they both seen and hated both me and my Father. But this cometh to pass, that the word might be fulfilled that is written in their law, They hated mewithoutacause.

The enemy will send storms to deter us from our destiny, but we can speak the Word to our storms and Goliaths and command them to move. The enemy's plan is really against God, but we are God's children, so he will try to get back at God any way he can. The enemy devises things against us that he is not able to carry out because of the blood of Jesus over our lives. The enemy works through people just as God does, but Jesus will do the separating at the harvest. We must try the spirit by the Spirit in us. We need to let God rise as the sun, and when he goes forth in his strength, the children of darkness shall be scattered as the shadows of the evening flee before the rising sun (Psalm 68 KJV).

We have a duty to pray for our enemy and those who speak against God. It was very hard for me to pray for my enemies at first, but it was the only way for me to be forgiven by God. I knew people who had bitter attitudes toward God and his Word, but that did not stop me from rejoicing because the joy of the Lord was my strength. It became instinctual for me to praise the one who had raised me up from paralysis. I loved calling the name of Jesus. He gave me my motion back by his spirit and defeated all my enemies. He gave me sufficiency in all things. Without him, I can do nothing. God's strength and power perfects me. He is a gracious God who is full of mercy and compassion.

God's power releases the pressure of all who try to oppress me. He gives it to orphans and widows. God gave me the liberty to call on him any time. He had pity on me and taught me and trusted me with his Word, and I started performing it. God blessed me and provided for me. He became my Father and my shepherd. He took care of all my complaints and opened his hand wide to meet my needs. God even made my hand happy with my finances. All I had to do was go into the secret place and he would give me comfort in my loneliness. I did not have to look anywhere else for relief; I just went into my medicine cabinet called the Bible and got all the relief I needed. Sometimes, I might have been down and out and broke, but God took care of me as he does the birds of the air.

God set me free from those who wanted to keep me in their bondage. Every time people did something wrong to me, something bad happened to them. They did not know that you reap what you sow. I received God's mercy, and they always made me remember that. We should never forget what God has done for us. I was guided by the Holy Spirit just as the Israelites in the wilderness were, and I had all I needed for the journey. I began to hear God's voice and see his glory in my life in Deuteronomy 4:32–33 (KJV).

> For ask now of the days that the past, which were before thee, since the day that God created man upon the earth, and ask from the one side of heaven unto the other, whether there hath been any such thing as the great thing is, or hath heard like it. Did ever people hear the voice of God speaking out of the midst of the fire, as thou hast heard and live?

God's amazing presence moved Mount Sinai (Judges 5:4–5; Deuteronomy 33:2; Habakkuk 3:3). That encourages our faith and our dependence on him. God will also move every mountain in your life and in the way of your happiness in God. God will help you in your Canaan as well as your wilderness. He will send rain and will be good to you. Remember how God sent manna and quails to the Israelites in the wilderness and milk and honey in Canaan. Deuteronomy 11:11 reads, "'But the land whither ye go to possess it is a land of hills and valleys and drinking water of the rain of heaven." God gave us spiritual provisions and the gospel of grace, which is the plentiful rain.

Isaiah 14:8 reads, "Yea the fir trees rejoice at thee, and the cedars of Lebanon saying, since thou art laid down no fellow is come up against us." God makes us victors because we have his sword to defeat all our enemies. The Lord gave us his Word, and great was the company that published it. God uses prophets and preachers to carry out his Word, and they have defeated kings without a blow. Jesus Christ's resurrection gave us authority over our spiritual enemies. We became overcomers by the blood of the Lamb and our testimonies. God brings us from poverty to prosperity. The Lord gives us peace from Satan and those that he uses to oppress us.

We should not be worried because God has assigned thousands of angels to our team. When Christ ascended to heaven, we became more than conquerors. Colossians 2:15 states, "And having spoiled principalities and powers, he made a shew of them openly, triumphing over them in it." Jesus broke the power of sin in our lives. This is what makes us more than conquerors through Christ Jesus. Jesus came in the flesh to observe his creation, and we need to get up close and personal with him.

Jesus found out that it was not easy being in the flesh, but he did so he would know how to give us victory over ourselves and the enemy. Romans 8:37 reads, "Nay in all these things we are more than conquerors through Him that loved us." Jesus opened heavens to all those who would believe. "Wherefore he saith when he ascended on high; he led captivity captive and gave gifts to men." Jesus gave humankind the chance to achieve eternal life with him. John 17:2–3 says,

> As thou has given Him power over all flesh that he should give eternal life to as many as thou hast given him. And this is life eternal, that they might know thee the only true God, and Jesus Christ, whom thou hast sent.

Jesus came in an earth suit so he would know how to give us the gifts we needed. He is a faithful high priest to us when he shows us his mercy. Jesus did all this for his hardheaded, rebellious, and disobedient children. His creation had to be renewed. "And you that were sometimes alienated and enemies in your mind by wicked works, yet now has the reconciled" (Colossians 1:21). Whenever a soul is saved, it blesses the kingdom of God. God came to a rebellious world not to condemn it but to save it.

God becomes a consuming fire to those who continually rebel against him. God set before man life and death, a blessing and a curse. He said, "Choose this day whom you will serve." Mark 16:16 says, "He that believeth and is baptized shall be saved, but he that believe not shall be damned." God has so many gifts for us that we will not have room to receive them all if we are obedient. He even loaded us with benefits. He is the God of our eternal salvation. We have a covenant relationship with God, but those who continue to fight him will be destroyed. Genesis 3:15 says, "And I will put enmity between thee and the woman, and between thy seed and her seed; it shall bruise thy head, and thou shalt bruise his heel." God's enemies like to be roaring lions, but they are only chihuahuas and puffs of smoke gone in a minute.

God will bring us out of deep trouble; he will lead us out of our wilderness into our Canaan. He will make us triumphant over our adversaries through Christ Jesus. He delivered me from my enemies; for some reason, they all just disappear. God clears our path by going before us. If we just stand in our position and rest in him, we will not have to fight but will receive victory.

Dogs will lick the blood of this rebellious, Jezebel, Antichrist generation. In Revelation 14:20, we read, "And the wine press was trodden without the city, and blood came out of the wine press, even unto the horse's bridles, by the space of a thousand and six hundred furlongs." That was a lot of blood. Those who assemble as believers see God's mighty power and strength. God is forming and strengthening us. He perfects whatever concerns us. When the unsaved see God working in our lives, that will lead them to God's house. They will come just from the fear of the Lord. I see so many attack God's people and refuse his teaching. They have many books but always the wrong books. The books they read do not feed their God-given spirits. They have knowledge but not biblical knowledge.

They will try to keep God's kingdom from advancing. Satan, the Lord rebukes you. I pray that the Lord cuts your pride off and lets the net that the proud have hidden catch them. I pray that they be overtaken by convictions of their conscience. I pray that they give up letting money be their god and let God be their source. I pray that they submit all to God in every situation so they can see the power of God.

Those who will not submit are putting on a show to make believers think they have it going on. They are really trying to keep from drowning in shame for the lives they have chosen. So they go to jail or stay away until they can make sin look good. They want to be worshipped like Satan to show us that they did not make the wrong choice. Some come in willingly when they see the destruction of their associates. When God speaks, we should listen. God wants to protect us, and we should have a reverent and worshipful fear of him. Sinners can't stand to see God's holiness. God gives us strength and power, but sinners live a lie because they won't worship God.

Sinners feel so worthless around saints because of the conflict, debate, and disharmony in their hearts. They will not understand that all comes from him and should be to him. Believers have none other than God to expect help and relief from. I thank you, Lord God, for your Word, your blood, and your name. We must use God's Word and hold onto his joy,

our strength. Joy is one of the strongest of the fruits of the Spirit, and we must have it in our lives. If we live according to God's Word and keep his commandments, we will receive whatever we ask for. We must answer the problems, situations, and troubles in our lives with the Word of God and make the devil flee.

Space

Once upon a time, there was a place called earth. Space is a place where the carnal mind is no longer operative. Some people who call themselves trekkies love space. They let their minds float around in space and imagine being on another planet. In the cocaine and crack world, they have phrases such as "Beam me up!" and "Let's go up!" Jehovah put man, who came from earth, in charge of earth.

Hollywood, in what I called "Lost" Angeles, is setting social standards for Americans. It is always said that anything that the mind can conceive can be done. NASA has sent probes to Mars and is working on a new probe called Insight, which will emit radio waves telling us how the planet rotates and information about its molten core and any liquid on the surface. (Google "NASA Insight.")

We have been watching the cartoon *The Jetsons* for our whole lives. We watched flying cars and escalators in the air and seeing one another talking on the phone, but I never imagined that it was going to happen. Man has had a desire to live in space for a long time. The Wright brothers made us think about air travel. God said that there would be wars and rumors of wars. Man is even getting set up for space wars. Right after man finishes destroying the earth with his very smart self, he will finish killing himself off in space. Wow! Isn't that exciting.

The Bible speaks about nuclear war. We associate nuclear weapons with Armageddon. Man has the capacity to wipe out much life on earth in a few hours. Those who survive will be looking for a new heaven and a new earth. Most human inventions backfire one way or another. Plastic bags seemed to be a good idea until it was discovered that they were hard to dispose of. Now, they dump plastic in the ocean and suffocate the fish. Satan always shows you the beginning, but he never tells you the end. This millennial generation is tearing up the earth. Isaiah 24:6 (Everyday Bible)

says, "The people of the earth have ruined it"; only a few will be left. They will set out in space to set up shop wherever they can being a generation so smart but without God to navigate their lives. God set the standard through his Word. This is a generation that worship what God created, not the creator. They are looking for some new air on another planet. When Jehovah breathed life into man, he became a living soul. Jehovah gave man every seed for fruit and for every green thing that we might need.

Jesus came into the world to keep us from self-destructing. The millennial generation seems to want to be anything but what God intended. Their imagination is stuck on electronics, which God made; they think more about creations than they do the creator.

Their parents did not teach them about God, so we have a generation that doesn't know God. They are accidents waiting to happen. Everything is set up for them, and they expect everything instantly. They all want to be bosses and kings, but none wants to serve long. Women want to be bosses, and men want to be kings. Their hearts are numb; they don't even know that when they are saved, they will become royalty—kings and queens and priests. The stage is being set for space travel, but people are being trained to live in front of a computer or cell phone. These are some of those who will miss the trip. They are still caught up in fear.

God wants us to love one another. He did not want us to isolate ourselves in a world of knowledge to become prey for those who write computer programs. Satan is the prince of the air waves. When you mention love, they run from it because there is no feeling in a relationship in electronics. People are being taken away from relationships with people and developing relationships with electronics. The prophecies are coming true. Man is still living a savage life and wants to take it to another planet. Ministers are sounding the trumpet, but man is going headstrong into self-destruction. The earth is man's one and only choice because when man leaves earth, no matter where he is, he still has to meet his maker. Everything else is just exploration. Now, man wants to go out and pollute the heavens.

Man is doing a lot of research trying to live longer. Young black kids are used in this research because of their healthy bodies. They are shot in the head to save vital body organs for rich people who put in orders for organs. All the killings are not just black-on-black crimes. There is a market for healthy young black vital organs mostly from black women. People are still trying to find the fountain of youth. Space explorers are like those who built the Tower of Babel. Man can stop trying to get to heaven in spaceships and just wait on his appointed time to die. In 1 Corinthians 15:52, we read, "In a moment, in the twinkling of an eye, at the last trump: the trumpet shall sound, and the dead shall be raised in corruptible and we shall be changed." They really want to go to heaven.

The Bible says that it is appointed once unto man to die. What man is looking for in space will happen to him because he is from eternity and will return to eternity. When Jesus returns, he will give us a new heaven and a new earth, so why would man want to take his cursed self out in space? They have already help curse the ground they came from, and now they want to spread the curse through the universe. No matter where you go, God is there. If a saved person went to Mars, God would be with him because he would be in him. If you get in right standing with Jehovah, you will have eternal life wherever you are.

Stop trying to get it yourself and just receive it by faith. God gave us all the necessities; all he wants from us is our obedience. We are from Jehovah, not space. Man wants to be like Jesus and ascend to heaven and come back to earth.

Satan always wanted to be boss. Now, the millennials want to be boss. Satan and his angels come as falling stars trying to get man to do their desires to get back in heaven. Satan uses man to irritate angels. Man is a pawn used by Satan to get back to heaven There is a spiritual war going on in heaven that man is not aware of.

"God is all, in all, and all in it." God said in 1 Corinthians 15:40–41, "Be not deceived: evil communication corrupts good manner: Awake to righteousness, and sin not; for some have not the knowledge of God: I speak this to your shame." Man wants to play God by creating life and wants to transfer to another planet ascending like Jesus. Man knows in part what he is doing, but what he doesn't know can make him a new world. "God's thoughts are higher than our thoughts." What man is looking for is right under his nose, but he won't open his Bible and read it to get the insight he needs. Instead, he sends probes called Insight to get insight.

God is ready to open the eyes of their understanding. God set Jesus at his right hand in heaven "far above all principalities, powers and might,

and dominion, and every name that is named, not only in this world, but also that which is to come" (Ephesians 1:20–21 KJV). When we get saved, God gives us everything we need.

The space travel that man wants is found in 1 Corinthians 15:40: "There are also celestial bodies, and bodies terrestrial: but the glory of the celestial is one, and the glory of the terrestrial is another." We have an earthly and a spiritual body in one. The bodies they are looking for in space happens after you die and leave that physical body. It will happen in a moment in the twinkling of an eye. The trekkies' idea of space will come to pass. God gave man a command: "Be fruitful and multiply, and replenish the earth, and subdue it: and have dominion over the fish of the sea, and over the fowls of the air, and over every living thing that moveth upon the earth," not space. We are going to have to be like the postage stamp on a letter and stick to God until we get there.

The Whole Duty of Man

We have heard the conclusion of the whole matter: fear God and keep his commandments; this is the whole duty of man. Praising God with the reverent and worshipful fear is our duty. We praise God by our obedience, praise, prayer, and worship and by witnessing to others. We always want God to do favors for us, but we don't want to do favors for God. Our favor to God is to show our appreciation to him by honoring him in praise and worship and being a vessel of honor through our obedience. This is part of the mystery of creation, and it is required of everything God made. Even the trees praise God. We should stop worshipping the things that God has made and worship God, who made them. "It is in him that we live and move and have our being."

We are brought from darkness into light, faith in Jesus Christ, to bless God because he holds our souls. He has the whole world in his hand. God gave us our being, and he guides us in our affairs as he continues to create in us his perfect will. God does not want us to just exist; he wants us to have joy in him because the joy of the Lord is our strength. God guides us from dangers seen and unseen and delivers us from distresses. God doesn't want us loaded down with problems; he wants us to be as carefree as Adam and Eve were in the garden of Eden.

God inhabits the praise of his people. When we go through afflictions, it seems we are going through fire. When I was in my affliction, I was just glad to be alive; I was thankful for his grace and the power of the Holy Spirit. We don't have to go through anything because everything we needed was done at the cross for us. Jesus gave us every victory we need. The enemy wants us to bow to him in defeat when God wants us to be victorious.

I can't see why men and women want to be wrong and stay wrong their whole lives. God designed us to keep the devil under our feet. God wants us to be holy as he is holy. We are refined by going through the fire and are made better by getting all our imperfections out. God wants to prove and improve us as silver in the fire bringing us closer to his likeness. His church will go through the fire and come out smelling like a rose. Whatever the trouble God's church may encounter, it will still bless him and he will make a way for it because of Jesus Christ, the head of the church. The church will be brought into a wealthy place, a well-watered garden bearing many fruits. God wants us to be fruitful and multiply. God does not want us to bear rotten fruit but fruit without spot or wrinkle. If we encourage one another, lift one another up, and share our experiences with each other as we wash each other's feet, God will be revealed in us. Every chance we get, we should tell each other how God has blessed us. When God blesses our souls, that shows him working in our lives. God is forming us into his image as we become Christlike. We feel more joy and have a need to pray and enlarge our hearts in prayer. David said, "I cried unto him with my mouth" (Psalm 66:17).

God gave us the privilege to pray. We must have a heart to pray and feel led to pray for ourselves, our nation, and those we encounter. When we extol or cry out to God, we raise him up. God is pleased when we humble ourselves with believing prayers from an upright heart. When we seek the welfare of others and ourselves, we seek his glory.

We should always think of ways to exalt and magnify Christ Jesus. When we pray, we should not leave off praise from our hearts. We should ask God to create in us clean hearts and renew our spirits. If we have any kind of iniquity in our hearts, God will not hear our prayers.

We must repent of our sin and then approach the throne of God. When we regard sin in our hearts, that is to say, if we have any agreement with sin, we become involved in it. If that happens, God will not entangle himself in our prayers and we will not have peace. If we agree with his Word and walk upright, God will show us his favor. So let's bless God when we win in our prayer life. God's mercy will deliver us.

We should know how to give glory to God in humble thankfulness. When God shows us his mercy and goodness, our "Praise waiteth for Him" (Psalm 65:1). We will receive his mercy and give him thanks. Praise makes me wait, and it gives me satisfaction to know God's will for my life while depending on his mercy. We must wait on the Lord and not murmur, complain, or doubt him.

I walk in what I believe, and my praise becomes silent because I am in his rest. I show my desire to receive his goodness. I speak words of faith to praise him. We must give God the glory for hearing our prayer. Our praise should be ever ready because God is always ready to grant us what we pray for. "God that hear our prayers can give us exceedingly, abundantly, above all that we can ask or think" (Ephesians 3:6). God answers every prayer of faith; we should take all our burdens to the Lord and leave them there. When we go through difficulties and our backs are against the wall,

we run to God, who hears our prayers. Our heads might be hanging low from the guilt of sin, but God forgives us if we repent. Micah 7:18 says, "Who is a God like unto thee, that pardons iniquity, and passeth by the transgression of the remnant of His heritage? He retains not His anger forever, because he delights in mercy." God's mercy is everlasting. Our sins make it to the heavenlies and separate us from God. Our iniquities take over our minds, and we become mentally kidnapped and make our consciences accuse us. A guilty conscience needs no accuser.

We should bless God because he takes all our transgressions away so we do not come into condemnation for them. We should stay plugged in to God so we can confess our sin and always be in right standing with him. Our sins must be purged before we can approach the altar of God. God allows everyone who is saved to approach him and converse with him as a friend. We can go in as the priest did and offer our prayers and petitions to God. God keeps us welcome in his house and listens to our requests. He wants to know how his children are doing.

God did not charge us to get into his house because salvation is free; isn't that nice? Jesus was the key who helps us get in, but it was his choice that we could come in. It was nothing that we did because salvation is free. "Blessed is the man whom thou hast chosen making them kings and priest in him, leaving those who will not repent for themselves." They serve themselves being their own gods with no supernatural power.

The good man will be satisfied with good things when he applies God's promises to his life by the fruit of his mouth. He will receive the goodness of God because he is part of his household. God keeps a good house, and he will not withhold anything from us. There is an abundance of goodness in God, enough for everyone. He has righteousness and grace abounding there. He has all the luxuries imaginable, and there are enough for every believer to receive some. He is ready to freely dispense them. God is ever ready to operate his power for his children and reward them for their obedience. Jehovah loves us.

God is righteous, and sometimes, he rebukes us by using terrible things to guide us and awaken and quicken us but always for righteousness's sake. It is like a shock treatment to get us back on track to our God-ordained destiny. God will take care of us. He is the God of all humankind but gives service to those who serve him or have a covenant with him. God renews us every morning and evening if we are plugged in to him.

God makes us rejoice when we wake up and when we go to sleep. When we lie down, we shall not be afraid. Our sleep will be sweet. God awakes us with new mercies in the morning that make us grateful to him. He closes the curtain in the evening, and we thank him for watching over us all day.

The joy of the Lord is our strength, and we should monitor our joy on the job and mirror joy to all we encounter. There is nothing like a sad Christian. How can we encourage others if we are not encouraged? We should stay in God's Word and let it water us and make us clean and fruitful just as he watered the earth and made it fruitful. Every good and perfect gift is from above. God blesses us by raining his righteousness on us. Psalm 65:9 says, "Thou visited the earth, and waters it: thou greatly enrich it with the river of God, which is full of water: thou prepare them corn, when thou hast so provided for it."

If our hearts are dry, we need God to water us just as he sends rain to water all the crops that nourish us. Just as water softens the ground for planting, God's Word softens the heart and makes it tender. God's Word establishes it with his grace if we are patient. When our springtime comes, it establishes our whole year and sets it in motion. God crowns with his goodness those who are faithful. He will send floods of goodness into our lives because he is good. We should not be selfish just for the things that concern us but for all God's creation.

Your Better Brings the Worst Against You

The better we get, the more others will envy us. This is the character of enemies as David described them: "Hear my voice O Lord in thy prayer: preserve my life from fear of the enemy" (Psalm 64). They are people who come after us with swords and bows. They are skillful men who talk secretly about us, and their words do not miss. Our success becomes their conversation. Their tongues are their swords, and their bitter words are their arrows.

They use abusive and vulgar language. They use disgraceful nicknames to make us feel less than who we are. They lie about us and slander us. They are deceitful. They target us and try to keep us down. The more we try to better ourselves, the more we are envied. They are cowardly backbiters afraid to face us directly. They throw rocks and hide their hands. They try to trap us with their words and talk poorly about us with others to harm us. This form of communication is of the enemy, Satan.

They think no one sees them, but God knows their whereabouts and what they are plotting. I say daily, "Let the net that he has hidden catch himself into that very destruction let him fall" (Psalm 35:8). I do all my lets in Psalm 35 morning and night. These are the people who don't believe in God; they put wickedness on their production line daily to see who can turn out the most wicked deeds. They plot day and night. Psalm 64:6 says, "They search out iniquity; they accomplish a diligent search; both the inward thought of every one of them, and the heart, is deep."

They love to find some iniquity in our lives; they will go back as far as our childhoods to lay charges on us. All the energy they put out to condemn us could have been put to much better use—to better their own lives and to gain deliverance. They go through a lot to pain those who are trying to better themselves and live in peace. One day, we were street evangelizing and one of the evangelists said about God haters, "They just want to be saved." Some people envy the just and upright because they can't see themselves being good with all the evil in them. They condemn our souls because they feel condemned.

God takes care of his people, and he will ordain his arrows to come against those who persecute us. God's arrows will come quicker on our enemies and will dig deeper into them bringing conviction. God goes before his people to clear the way for their success. We should look at Paul, who persecuted the church, and how God dealt with him. God has a way of making our tongues fall on ourselves. Words that were meant to hurt saints will bounce off them and boomerang to the one who spoke them.

We should stay away from such negative backstabbers. They want to influence our judgment of others. When they are exposed, they run away because they are cowards. We should not worry because the finger of God will punish our persecutors. This goes around in our homes, churches, and in every other area of our lives. Good people should take notice of this because the righteous should be glad in the Lord.

God's people have chosen life while the devils' crowd has chosen death. Our job is to glorify God and his Word and let it be fulfilled in our lives. When the enemy tries to injure the innocent, we should recite Psalm 35:1– 2: "Plead my cause O Lord with those who strive with me. Fight against those who fight against me. Take hold of shield and buckler and stand of for my help." Put the icing on it with Psalm 91. Don't forget your benefits in Psalm 103, and have a happy whatever day it is, and stay the best!

According to Psalm 62, we should not have confidence in unfaithful man but in faithful God. A lot of people are leaving the church because they are not walking in the spirit but in the flesh. If they were in the spirit, they would not be looking at man but at God. When we go to church, we should ask ourselves what we are looking for—God's presence or others' approval. God's church is built on a rock that will stand, but those who fight against it shall fall like a building with no foundation.

We have to be a hundred percent all day to defeat our adversary. We can't put our trust in the men or women of this world whether they are rich or poor. They may be too poor to help us, but God is our source. They may try to deceive us if we trust in them. They use drugs to throw us off course and manipulation to try to get us to bow down to the works of Satan. We must try the spirit by the spirit and lay them in the balance of scripture and test or prove them to see if they are the kind of persons we are looking to share our company with. See if they answer your expectations of them. "Thou are weighed in the balance and are found wanting." We should not trust in wealth gotten by fraud or oppression. With all the technology on earth, how could we not know that Jesus's blood covers us? "For there is no respect of persons with God" (Romans 2:11).

ABOUT THE AUTHOR

Steven Treadwell is a noted author and minister chosen by God to encourage, uplift, and motivate those he comes in contact with to read the unadulterated, uncompromising, unchanging Word of God. He was born in Memphis, Tennessee, where he graduated from George Washington Carver High. He started to serve God at an early age being baptized at age ten.

He sung in the choir at church and in junior high school, high school, and college. He studied sociology and sang in the college choir under Omar Robinson, a music maestro, for a year and a half at Shelby State (now called Southwest Tennessee College). He transferred from Shelby State to Philander Smith in Little Rock, Arkansas, where he continued studying sociology and singing in the choir.

His mission has always been to motivate others to share their courage and confidence. He moved to Los Angeles and studied the teachings of Fredrick K. Price at Crenshaw Christian Center, where he began to walk by faith, not by sight, and he was not afraid of what he saw or heard and became very conscious of what he said.

He studied real estate briefly at West Los Angeles in Culver City. He was in the city of angels with a devil's heart and didn't take that lightly. While working across from CBS on Beverly Blvd and Fairfax, he rubbed shoulders with the stars, who gave him a larger-than-life picture of himself. His job delivering flowers kept him on the scene in LA, and then he moved to Atlanta to attend Rutledge, a small business college.

He reached out to save a struggling school but was too late. He returned to Memphis after sharing what he had learned at Crenshaw

Christian Center in Atlanta. He studied more and evangelized at Northwest College in Southhaven, Mississippi, the University of Phoenix, Strayer University, and the University of Memphis.

He is writing his second book and still providing others a reason to do everything with courage and confidence.

www.ingramcontent.com/pod-product-compliance
Lightning Source LLC
Chambersburg PA
CBHW070713130626
46553CB00005B/1964